Natural
For Beginners

The Essential DIY Guide With 62 Homemade Soap
Recipes For Cold & Hot Process, Liquid, Melt-and-
pour & Hand-milled. Includes How To Make Money
From Home Selling Soap

By

Grace Flowers

Table of Contents

Foreword

Soap making is an age-old tradition, which has almost vanished due to the availability of commercial soaps. While people from yesteryears didn't have a choice but to make their own soap, more people these days are opting for handmade soaps as a natural alternative to chemical-rich, store-bought soaps.

What most people don't know about soap is that it's actually salts. If you still remember your high school chemistry, you'll know that salt is a product of the chemical reaction between an acid and a base. Indeed, soap is made from an animal or plant-derived fats and oils (which are acids) and lye (which is a base).

The craft of making natural soaps in the comfort of your own home is becoming more and more popular today, and it's easy to see why. The question is, is it worth making your own soap at home rather than simply picking one from the grocery store ready to use? Of course, I'd say yes! But let me support this answer. Below, I listed down some of the benefits of homemade soap.

- **You Are Avoiding Chemicals**

Even though most brands we find in the market today have a

list of ingredients they use to make their products, you can't tell for sure how accurate they are – you don't know what's really in there! On the other hand, because you're making your own soap, it all depends on you what ingredients you want to use.

- **You Are Using Real Soap**

You have to keep in mind that most of the soaps you can buy in the market are mass-produced. It's also common to find "soap" that is labeled as whitening soap, body deodorant, and the like. These are simply chemical concoctions made of cleansers and absolute alarming synthetic ingredients that may cause early skin aging, allergic reactions, and some of which that have been linked to numerous types of cancer.

- **You Have Endless Options**

If you're a fan of variety, then look no further as doing it DIY at home will provide you with just what you needed! Regardless of what type of skin you have or what your personal preferences are, you can create something according to your needs.

- **You Save Money**

Okay, this one probably surprised you. Contrary to popular belief, making homemade soap is cheaper than simply buying ones.

If you're a fan of variety, then look no further as doing it DIY at home will provide you with just what you needed! Regardless of what type of skin you have or what your personal preferences are, you can create something according to your needs.

Ready to get started?

Grace Flowers

Introduction

Soap sold commercially is most often made on a large scale with the most cost-effective way possible. This includes using chemical detergents, hardening material and other chemicals that are very harmful to your skin.

The chemicals in commercial soap often leave your hands dry as they focus on cleaning and forget about pampering your skin. When you make homemade soap, it is made with natural ingredients such as lye and natural oils.

Moreover, you can also control what you add in there, for example, adding natural aromatherapy oils or compounds such as glycerin. Glycerin is a small amino acid that is very good for the softness of your skin.

The process of soap making naturally produces glycerin. However, most commercial soaps don't have glycerin. That is because they extract it to make use of it for other skin loving and high-quality products such as moisturizing lotions. This leaves the soap hard and irritating to the skin, although it cleans well. But soap also needs to be skin loving and soft on the skin. With natural homemade soap, you can add glycerin or whatever skin friendly ingredient you want to add.

You may argue that homemade soap uses lye and you don't want lye on your skin. The wonder of chemistry is that during the process of saponification, the lye completely dissolves and reacts with the oils used to form soap, and no more lye remains if you have used the correct proportions.

One of the best advantages of making your own soap is that you can be sure of all the ingredients included. You are 100% in control. You can choose to use all-natural products, even the coloring can be used from natural and skin friendly alternatives.

Another beauty of making your own soap is that you are the master of the process. You can control how you want your soap to feel. Do you want to make it soft or hard? What scent do you want your soap to have?

Do you want your soap to be frothy and lathery or have little lather? All this you can control by adjusting the proportions of lye and the type of oils you use.

For example, using castor oil gives you different results than when using olive oil and so on and so forth. The possibilities are almost endless with homemade soap. Think of all the experimenting fun you can have!

Soap making can be a life changing activity. DIY soap is a fun and relaxing activity to do to release stress. Therefore, it is a great outlet to de-stress and try something new. It is also an outlet to feel different or discover a new hobby. It is a great opportunity to express and discover your creativity by experimenting with different proportions, ingredients and add ones.

Moreover, you can always get creative with the shapes of the molds, color combinations, petal additions and even the final packaging. It would also be perfect as a bonding arts and crafts activity. Your homemade soap will make you feel proud about your achievement and progress as you can see your bathroom shelves stacked with the magical work of your hands.

Soap making can also be your chance to increase your income as you can make handmade soap and sell it, making your own brand by using your own creative touch. Homemade soap has helped a lot of females take care of their families by selling the soap they make. Moreover, it is a creative and a wonderful sensual gift to give your friends, family or loved ones.

There are tons of reasons to make your own soap!

PART I: SOAP MAKING 101

Chapter 1: The Origins Of Soap Making

The creation of soap was likely accidental and beneficial to humanity. The prevalent story says livestock were burnt as sacrifices to gods on Mount Sapo. The fire pits were full of debris and animal fats after the rituals. When it rained, the ashes and fats washed into the mud, bringing them down to the river. As the women brought their washing to the shore, clumps of a thin, waxy powder were discovered floating in the stream. The people were washing their garments by pounding rocks on them. This made a lather as the waxy material was pounded with the clothing, and cleaner was the cloth. It was finally figured out, and the purposeful method of producing soap began.

When lye (then a powerful alkaline solution extracted from wood ashes to transform fats into soap) became commercially accessible, soap making became a routine activity. Women saved fat drippings and created soap from them later. This magnificent soap making event was an activity that took place once a year, sometimes with several housewives participating in the task. The soap was rough and gritty at times and was used to clean up everything.

The phrase "grandmother' lye soap" always strikes terror into many people who were raised early in the last century. Never be afraid; today's homemade lye soaps, manufactured in carefully managed quantities, bear no similarity to what your grandma would have used to wash out the mouth of your father when he was a child.

As with every labor-intensive job, soap making became a threat to the busy housewife's limited time and energy. The industrial revolution, which, on a large scale, transformed the Western world, has had a significant effect on the everyday life of people who cared for households and families. Huge relief was provided by washing machines, advanced cooking stoves, vacuum cleaners, and running water. Goods that were previously manufactured primarily at homes such as cotton, fiber, fabric, and clothes were produced largely and could be bought at reasonably affordable rates in stores.

Technological developments have also been extended to soap manufacturing as fairly priced cheap toilets, and house-cleaning soaps were easily accessible.

Likewise, at an appealing price-benefit ratio, all were available: inexpensive all-purpose soaps and costly bathroom cleaner, and all in between. Because the strength of lye made from wood ash has been difficult to control, soap making at home was a labor of some trials and errors. Thus, others depended on town chandlers, or candle makers, who produced soap too.

Chandlers gathered fat from housewives for cooking and butchering, produced soap, and marketed it back to home wives. The soap was expensive, however, and thrifty housekeepers tended to produce soap at home.

Like in so many other issues, soap making automation and convenience in many ways needed sacrifice. However, largely produced soap is quite long-lasting and has everything of good consistency lost, scent, form, and color. Any connection to the soap making process, along with the glycerin, is eliminated from commercial soap.

A Brief History Of Soap And Soap Making

The "new" soap as it is known to be, wasn't created until 600 AD. Soap-making factions were developed at this period too. Perhaps to refresh your mind, a faction was a community of traders or craftsmen who have ensured that their art values are maintained.

In the early 800s, soap making craft factions were especially common in Spain and eventually became the leading soap manufacturer in the Western world. This wasn't until around 400 years back, about 1200 AD, that England took charge of soap manufacturing. This was attributed to the observation of a French scientist, Nicolas Leblanc.

In the late 1700s, he found that lye could be extracted from table salt before even today as a main component of soap.

Many soap makers label the onset of modern handcrafted soap making renaissance with Ann Bramson's 1972 publishing of a small book, named Soap. Ever since, soap making has developed considerably in art, design, hobby, and industry, and people around the world are experiencing the same pleasure that those legendary washerwomen of Mount Sapo would have felt when they found the delight of handmade soaps.

World War 1 contributed to the usage of synthetic detergents, and the scarcity of easily available animal fat demanded a particular supply of fatty acids for homemade soap. To this purpose, we use vegetable oils today. Moreover, the ashes used throughout history were modified, and the active ingredient extracted and today we use sodium hydroxide.

For hundreds of years, people have produced soap to help clean dirt and oil from their bodies, dishes, surfaces, floor, or clothes. Individuals have needed to produce soap at home in the past, as it was not available in stores. At home, soap making was a time-consuming, messy, and hot procedure that many people performed only once a year.

Currently, the industrial soap that you and your family are using follows a standard formula and is also being manufactured in a pretty close manner as it was about a hundred years earlier, shortly after the industrial revolution. However, the ways the producers have changed involve rendering soap milder on the skin, soap coloring, and its scent.

How Soap Products Became Popular

Entrepreneurs in many geographical regions have established factories to produce specialized soaps with a transparent type with a distinctive and delicate fragrance.

Since people also needed laundry soap, manufacturers started grinding soap with a mortar and pestle to make flakes that rapidly dissolved in warm water. By the late 18th century, soap making became a huge business with the opening of large industries in major cities. Many of those industries still operate today, producing various soaps and laundry types. Intensive advertisement for soap in newspapers and magazines caused individuals to buy soaps in retail shops quickly.

Chapter 2: Introduction To Soap Making

Soap Making can be as creative as your imagination allows. I will help you start by sharing basic recipes and building your confidence until you are experimenting and creating soaps on your own. If you've always wanted to make goat milk and honey soap, then you're in luck.

How about Castile soap, soap for sensitive skin, or soap for babies? I've included a lot of specialty soaps like shampoo bars, shaving bars, and soaps made with essential oils that are known to help calm allergies.

I've even included camping soaps like a jewelweed soap to help prevent poison ivy and poison oak reactions and an insect-repelling soap with citronella and other essential oils that combine to make a pleasant aroma for you, but an effective deterrent for bugs.

Maybe you're interested in soap because you're creative and want to make beautiful soaps with layers, stripes, and swirls. I'll give you the techniques to make sure you are ready to explore your artistic side. Remember, even if I give you step-by-step instructions for natural coloring and scents, you can always mix and match ideas from other recipes.

Scents and colors are easy to substitute. Oils are a bit trickier, needing some calculations, but I'll show you how to do substitutions so that you'll be making your own recipes by the time you are finished.

What Is Soap?

There's no better way to understand something than to make it, but without background knowledge you can sometimes feel a bit lost. Which is why I can't teach you how to make soap without first answering the fundamental question: What is soap? Put simply, when lye water is added to oils, there is a chemical reaction called saponification.

Just as your elementary school vinegar and baking soda volcano eruption demonstrated a chemical reaction when two Ingredients came together to make something completely different, the saponification process is a chemical reaction between fatty acids (oils, butters, fats) and sodium hydroxide (lye) that makes something new: soap. Recipes are developed with the goal of using all the lye during saponification so that no lye remains in the final soap product.

People have been making soap for centuries. Farmers would use every part of their animals, including the fat, to make things like candles and soap.

Later, certain regions became famous for their olive oil and laurel berry oil soaps. My grandmother used to make soap with her mother using potassium hydroxide, or what she called potash, by taking the ashes from the fire, mixing it with straw, and running water through it for a few weeks.

This would create a strong enough liquid to react with the fats they had saved to make a soft soap that they would scoop out of a tin and use on dishes, clothes, and even their bodies. Using these same age-old principles with a modern method, you'll soon be doing this kind of science in your own kitchen.

The Benefits Of Making Your Own Soap

Before you dive into any new project, it's helpful to understand the benefits of what the project will provide. When it comes to soap making, there are huge benefits to making your own from scratch.

You Know The Ingredients

This is the most important benefit for me and my family. When you make your own soap from scratch, you know exactly what is going into it. You make the decisions on what is healthy for your skin and for the skin of those you love. No processing procedure or GRAS Ingredients (Ingredients that the government determines to be "generally recognized as safe" and thus do not need to be listed on a label) are getting into your soap because you are in full control.

Even homemade soap makers may fall into the trap of using fragrance oils and pigment powders. In my opinion, why go to all the trouble of making something with wonderfully nourishing oils, only to ruin it by adding toxic Ingredients?

You do not have to compromise quality. Instead, you will have fewer problems and difficulties in making your soap because, more often than not, it is artificial Ingredients that cause botched batches.

Health Benefits

Your skin is the largest organ on your body, and it is extremely absorbent. The products that you put on your skin affect your overall health. When you make soap from scratch, you not only know your Ingredients, but you control them. You can add essential oils for aromatherapy benefits, as well as clays, charcoal, and herbs to address acne and other skin concerns.

Saving Money

If you want to be healthy, buying premade organic and premium products can become really expensive. When you make your own, there is an initial cost to the ingredients, but once you have them on hand, you can make enough soap for family and friends and still have ingredients left over to make lotions, lip balms, and other bath and body products.

Self-Sustainability

One of the reasons I started writing this book, was because I wanted to learn and share how to make more of what we use on a daily basis. I value being able to have the choice to buy or make my own products.

Soap, shampoo bars, shaving bars, laundry bars—these are all things that we use on an almost daily basis and that we can create ourselves.

Pride and Satisfaction

There is something very exciting about making a beautiful batch of soap with your own hands. It'll get you hooked, in a good way. My first batches were made with makeshift molds, and the results were funky shapes and sizes. I still couldn't have been prouder. I was like a little girl making her first batch of cookies. I still feel the same way today.

Learning a Marketable Skill

Many people today are searching for pure and natural bath and body products. Who knows? You could end up starting a very successful home business, just as I did.

The Basics Of Soap Making

Soap Making from scratch can seem confusing at first, but I like to break the process down into categories and simplified steps.

The steps you see here are the same steps you will see in the recipes. An understanding of what is happening at the molecular level will also help you visualize each step and why it is necessary.

The Science Of Soap Making

For saponification, you need long-chain fatty acids (oils, butters, fats) and sodium hydroxide (lye). Every oil has a unique combination of three fatty acids attached to a glycerol. This is why each soap recipe calls for more than one oil: each oil brings a different combination of fatty acids and reacts with the lye differently. A soap made from multiple oils will have multiple benefits—like moisturizing, conditioning, and cleansing. When the lye and fatty acids are mixed together, the fatty acids release glycerol molecules that bond with the lye. This chemical reaction creates soap (technically a salt). The glycerin releases when you use it and nourishes your skin.

The Process Of Soap Making

It's helpful to think of a soap recipe in three parts.

1. Oils And Fats

You will weigh the oils, fats, and waxes in your recipe, melt them together, and then let the mixture cool to around 110°F.

2. Lye Water

After measuring the lye and water separately, you will pour the lye into the water. Do this outside! Be sure to read the "Safety First" section in the book and follow those steps carefully to have a safe soap making experience. Once combined, allow the mixture to cool to around 110°F.

3. Essential Oils And Other Natural Additives

After everything is cooled to around 110°F, you will pour the lye water into the oils and blend until trace. Trace occurs when the soap mixture thickens enough that when you drizzle some over the top of your mixture with a spoon, you can see a trace, or trail. This is often when scents and colors are added, though sometimes colors are added to lye water or oils.

Essential oils and fragrance oils may be added into your own soaps to provide it a curative impact. Some crucial oils like chamomile can be somewhat pricey.

Online e-Label Record

USPS Tracking Number:

9202 0902 3408 1501 3804 69

First-Class Package Return® Service

Print Date: 4/3/2021

From: Heather Polo
19195 Brookfield Rd
Chagrin Falls OH 44023

To:
Stride Rite / ODW
1 COLLECTIVE WAY
BROOKVILLE OH 45309-9901

QR Code Instructions

Scan QR Code to Request Free Package Pickup
or to Find a Post Office to drop off Packages

1. Center the label onto the largest side of the package so that the label information does not wrap around any edge.

2. If not using a self-adhesive label, tape or glue shipping label to the package. DO NOT TAPE OVER BARCODE. Be sure all label edges are secured.

3. DO NOT PHOTOCOPY. Each shipping label number is unique to the intended shipment and can be used only once. If needed, contact merchant for replacement label.

4. If reusing box or container, remove, cover, or mark out completely any other barcode and address markings.

5. Mail the parcel at a Post Office, drop it in a collection box, leave it with a letter carrier or schedule a free carrier pickup at usps.com

UNITED STATES
POSTAL SERVICE   *Thank you for shipping with the United States Postal Service!*

It truly is all up to you in the event that you wish to incorporate essential oils into your own soap. If you would like to just add a scent with no curative impact, then you can elect to utilize fragrance oils rather.

Blossoms and flower petals may add scent to an own soap, but you ought to keep in mind that these may be burnt when added to warm processed soap. Various other herbs don't seem at all attractive once used in soaps. If you would like to use herbs on your home soap, then do your research and discover out what herbs are great to be used in creating soap.

Glitter may be employed to bring a particular punch to your home soaps. Use cosmetic grade glitter; those arrive in ultrafine and fine dimensions and at a huge array of colors. Don't use glitter made to be used in craft projects since they aren't supposed to be utilized in skin.

4. Trimming And Cutting

When the soap you made is completely hard, the next step to follow is cutting and curing it. Before you can cut your soap to size, the first thing to take into consideration is the size you have in mind for the soap bar.

On average, a soap bar is usually about three-quarters of an inch thick, anything thicker than this and this user of the soap bar might have quite a hard time handling such a bar in the bath or shower.

If you are interested in having a soap bar that is evenly sized, simply measure the soap block when it is removed from the mold and cut each soap bar evenly. Some cutters make use of wire, I have seen people make use of guitar string wire as a cutter, this is usually used to cut soap bar into size by pulling it tightly across two wood pieces.

You can visit the nearest hardware store to buy a very sharp long knife or a cutter to with patterns - this will lead to patterned soap.

Once the soap bars have been cut to size, you can proceed with storing the soap in an area that is well ventilated for four to six weeks to allow it to complete the saponification process and dry evenly. Make sure you turn the soaps over every other day in bids to make it dry evenly.

Don't Be Afraid To Experiment

Knowledge of components in addition to imagination and creativity is necessary as soon as you understand the way to make homemade soap so as to make something that's really unique. When making your own soap, do your homework and also don't be afraid to try new items. As always, safety comes first, so let's discuss some safety considerations while making soap at home.

Chapter 3: Safety Guidelines

You may have heard that soap making can be dangerous, and maybe at the hands of a very careless person, that could be, but honestly, that is true for just about anything. The art of soap making does not need to be a scary or intimidating process.

All you need is a good understanding of the materials you are using and a few safety precautions. As you begin making soaps, you will develop your own routine that fits your style, and soon you will be crafting soaps like a pro.

As you are starting out, and as you continue to grow and develop your new skill, it is important that you always keep the following pieces of safety advice in mind.

Take care of yourself first. This means making sure that you are wearing all of the necessary protective gear including sturdy shoes that will protect your feet from spills, long pants to cover your legs, an apron to protect your clothes, long heat-resistant gloves, safety glasses, and a hat or hair tie to keep your hair out of your face. It is also wise to keep precautionary first aid items handy in case of an accident. These could include bandages, burn cream, and vinegar to neutralize any area of the skin that lye comes in contact with.

Make sure that you have all of your equipment ready to go. Make sure that you have read your formula, know exactly what you need, and have premeasured as much as possible. Having everything set up will make the process easier for you and will eliminate potential errors along the way.

Don't be afraid of lye but do treat it with respect and caution. Lye is poisonous and potentially fatal if ingested. The fumes can also be irritating to the eyes, skin, and lungs. Always use lye properly, keep it away from your face, work in a well-ventilated space, and keep the poison control number nearby, just in case.

Lye is reactive with aluminum, tin, and copper, so it is important to make sure that none of your tools that will come into contact with the lye are made from these materials.

When possible, choose the pellet form of lye, which is easy to use, over the powdered form, which can produce a lye cloud if you are not careful. Choose heat-resistant glass, stainless steel, silicone, and wooden pieces of equipment.

There is a chemical reaction that occurs when water and lye meet. It is a safer practice to add the lye to water than it is to add the water to lie. Keep in mind that lye reactions produce heat and be prepared to handle your utensils in the same way that you would if you were cooking. Keep commonsense in mind, even when you become comfortable.

After your first couple of batches of soap making, you will realize how incredibly easy it is to do, and as you become more comfortable, it can be easy to let some commonsense approaches to safety slide. For example, making soap can be a family activity, but extreme caution should be used when children are involved. Make sure that children are adequately protected, and keep the soap making for older children only. Younger children who are impulsive and unpredictable present a very serious risk for themselves and anyone else if allowed in the soap making area. Always keep your area well ventilated. Never leave your soap unattended during the process, and work in an area and at a time when you know you will be free of distractions. A little prevention in these areas will go a long way in keeping your soap making safe and enjoyable.

Safety is always first. Working with Lye and inducing a chemical reaction entails taking caution when attempting such procedures.

Understand Your Ingredients

Before you start, it is highly advised that you take your time to do some research about your ingredients, to understand exactly what are you working with.

For example, lye is a substance to be treated with care. Spend some time getting to know about it for example, if you spill lye solution, don't attempt to neutralize it with vinegar. Instead, you need to rinse it with excess water. Whether it splashed in your eyes or mouth or on your skin, rinsing it with water is the only and best solution to avoid skin or eye injury. If it spills on your clothes, remove the affected clothes immediately.

Follow Your Recipe

Chemical reactions need to occur in a certain way. It is all about proportions. Too much or too little of something can result in an undesirable effect.

In soap making, all recipe Ingredients are mentioned by weight, often ounces as you use traces of each ingredient.

Therefore, it would be great if have your recipe printed-out so you can make sure of it, instead of fumbling with the phone or tablet while working with your Ingredients, especially lye, you might risk spilling something. It may take you a couple of times to memorize the recipe by heart and then it would be much easier.

The second thing you need to follow your recipes precisely is a sensitive scale. Get a good quality kitchen scale or a digital scale. Make sure you test it out first with other known weights, such as a coin of known weight to confirm your balance's accuracy.

Once tested, you need to weigh out all your Ingredients as per your recipe. It is not advised to alter to change anything in the beginning. Some recipes mention percentages rather than weights which you can use to modify recipes according to your desired quantity but in the beginning, it is best to test with a prewritten recipe.

Take Care Of Your Eyes

Your eyes should be one of your number one safety priorities. A lot of things could go wrong and enter your eye during soap making. However, you can overcome this problem by wearing safety lab goggles. Lye or raw soap or dye powder all could find their way into your eyes, but not if you had safety goggles on. You should never skip this step.

You also need close-by access to water to wash it just in case. If you want maximum visibility, consider anti-fog goggles.

Take Care Of Your Skin

Just like your eyes, the same is true for your skin. Lye or raw soap can be highly irritant to your skin if you were not wearing protective gloves.

You can use latex gloves or rubber gloves. Dishwashing gloves are also fine, but they can be bulky to work with.

You could also protect your skin by wearing an apron or long-sleeved top so that you don't have your skin exposed.

Ventilate Your Room

It is not advisable to work with a chemical reaction and the raw soap smell with closed windows. Keep the windows opened in the room that you are in to breathe fresh air.

Be Prepared for Spills

Even if you wear protective gear, anything could happen. That is why it is always important to have a plan B. Buy a granular absorbent or a universal absorbent spill kit and have this nearby. The spill could be oil, your soap, lye, etc. Always keep a water supply nearby.

Make Sure You Have Printed the Right Recipe Without Any Errors

Sometimes people can write anything on the Internet without having the appropriate knowledge of the percentages and calculations. Make sure you get recipes from trusted sources.

Prepare All Your Ingredients Before Hand

When you start, there isn't then time to go around your kitchen gathering or weighing the rest of your Ingredients. Keep everything ready and within hands reach before you start.

Work With A Clear Space

Clutter is always a huge obstacle in any process. With lots of clutter, the chances of error increase. Always keep a clear working space.

Record Your Results And Learn From Your Mistakes

It is important to record the results of your batches so that you can figure out what went wrong and avoid it in the future.

- Keep Pets and Children Away
- Label the Utensils You Used for Lye
- Be cautious but don't let that inhibit your creativity to decrease your fun

Safety When Working With Lye

Lye is one of the key Ingredients for anyone who may be working with soap. However, in order to be safe around lye, you need to understand how to use it and what kind of equipment you will need to keep on hand as you work.

The reason why is because it is extremely corrosive. It is very dangerous both for your skin and for your eyes, and should of course never be swallowed or deeply breathed in. To start ensuring that you are truly safe around lye, make sure that family members are at a distance, and that there are no children or pets nearby. If there does happen to be someone else working with you on the production of soap, make sure that they are also wearing all of the necessary protective equipment.

Gloves

High-quality gloves are essential when you are working with the liquids that go inside soap. Make sure that you get the proper laboratory gloves that go all the way up to your elbows. They need to be able to cover a large surface of your skin, so that you can stay protected in case any splashes occur while you work.

Goggles

Another piece of very important equipment are of course goggles. Since we mentioned that lye is very dangerous for your eyes, you need to protect them with the help of professional goggles. Once again, choose the ones that would be used in laboratories, because they are the most likely to have the high standard of quality that can truly protect your eyes.

Protective Clothing

As you work on developing your own style of soap, there will almost certainly be splashes and mistakes along the way, and you really need to make sure that you prepare for them so that you don't suffer any injuries. In order to do this, you need to make sure that the clothing you are wearing is the kind that will be able to protect you against accidental burns.

Choose clothes that have thick textures, with long sleeves and long pants. Also, make sure that you are not wearing slippers, but instead ensure that you are wearing proper shoes that will also protect your toes.

Face Mask

A good face mask will protect you from any fumes that may be coming up from your soap mixture. This is especially important if you have any kind of allergies or perhaps asthma. You need to ensure that you protect your lungs from any substances that might cause them harm. This is especially true if you intend to be working on soap for a long period of time, because small injuries here and there could eventually pile up into a serious problem.

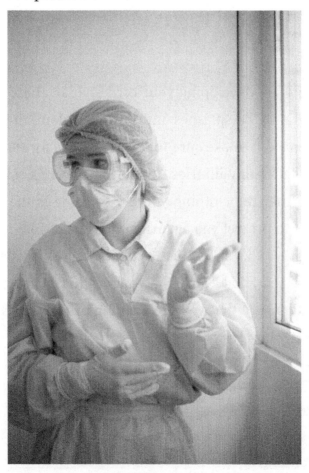

Chapter 4: Equipment, Safety Gear and Ingredients

Equipment and Molds

For an easy and successful production of homemade soap, you will need the following simple equipment.

- **Weighing scale**

This is about the most important equipment required for the successful production of soap at home. The usual kitchen scale isn't recommended because the chemicals require precise measurement in order for the soap to come out perfectly. Therefore, a sensitive scale that is digital in nature should be acquired.

- **Thermometer**

It is required because the temperatures of the different Ingredients may differ. Therefore, it is of utmost importance that the temperature of the raw materials used be controlled so as to obtain a good product at the end of the process. The recommended thermometer is an infrared thermometer, although cheaper alternatives can be very useful.

- **Containers**

Containers for mixing the chemicals and the soap mixture. These have to be plastic in nature to forestall a chemical reaction between the raw materials and the containers. The size of the soap to be produced will determine the size of the plastic containers.

- **Plastic spoons or a spatula**

This is used to scoop the raw materials for weighing.

- **Measuring containers**

This is used to measure the oil or oils and the lye before mixing them together to get the soap.

- **Stick for turning**

Optional - hand mixer or immersion blender. Depending on your financial capabilities, you can opt for a hand mixer for better product outcomes; otherwise, a wooden or plastic stick will suffice for mixing the oil and lye to make the soap.

- **Soap molds**

Any rectangular containers can be used as molds. These should be oiled wooden molds or plastic in nature so that the chemical doesn't react with the mold.

The mold is used to shape the soap after production after which it can be cut into smaller pieces.

In fact, there are three types of molds one can get for beginners - silicon molds, wood molds, and plastic molds.

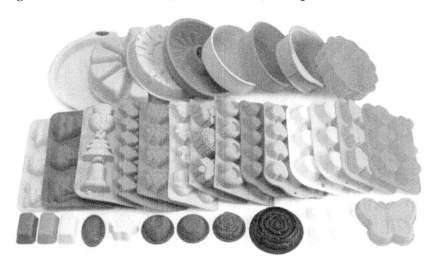

The wood molds should be lined with freezer paper or silicon liner before use. For the soap to come out cleanly and quickly always oil the surface lightly before pouring the soap into the mold.

Safety Gear

While the production of soap at home is generally considered a safe process, the use of protective gear cannot be overemphasized. This includes gloves, goggles, and a face mask for safety. This equipment is very essential for safety. Lye is very corrosive and should be handled with care. Hence while handling lye always make sure to use gloves and goggles to prevent injury to your hands and eyes. Use gloves and goggles that are specifically made to be used when working with chemicals. Use a face mask to cover the nose and mouth region to prevent caustic soda splashing into the nostrils and mouth.

- **Plastic boots**

To protect your feet in case of spillover

- **A coverall or apron**

It should be worn over clothing.

This will not only protect the individuals from injury but also will protect the inner clothing from being damaged by spills from the chemicals.

- **Strainer and funnel**

This may be necessary at times for the measurement of the chemicals and oil. The strainer will remove any particles present in the chemical which might not be visible as solid but present after dissolving them while the funnel is used to decant the liquids neatly while measuring them with measuring containers.

- **A lye calculator**

It may be required to help calculate the quantities of lye required for the production of soap.

- **A blender**

Useful for grinding herbal components and other soap additives.

- **Stamps to be used on the soap**

This is important if you hope to sell your homemade soaps. This can be obtained from your local artist who might be able to design one to your satisfaction. After the production of the soap, this stamp is used to impress and mark the soap with your own identity.

- **Working surfaces made of wood or plastic**

If you opt for a wooden surface, you need to cover the surface with a PVC table mat to prevent the lye from damaging the wood. NOTE: The plastic to be used in production should have recycled #5. Never use glass or aluminum containers in the production of soap.

Soap Making Ingredients

- **Oils or fat**

Several oils can be used to produce beautiful homemade soap.

Here they are: olive oil, coconut oil, palm oil, shea butter, cottonseed oil, castor oil, avocado oil, peanut oil, soybean oil, jojoba oil, tallow or lard.

- **Lye**

This may be potassium hydroxide or sodium hydroxide.

- **Water**
- **Fragrance oils**

These are essential oils which leave the soap with a good fragrance at the end of the production. Their usage is optional.

- **Color**

It is optional.

- **Preservatives**

They are necessary to keep the soap from being infected with bacteria or fungi during storage. Grapefruit extract, carrot root oil, and Tocopherols are natural preservatives that could be used in soap making.

- **Herbal additives**

These include aloe Vera, balsam, honey, oatmeal, alfalfa meal, seaweed.

Chapter 5: Soap Making Methods

There are five different ways that you go about creating your own soaps. Two of these methods involve starting from scratch and promoting the chemical reaction that changes other substances into a new soap. The other two methods involve taking already existing soaps and recreating them into something new. As you begin soap making you may wish to experiment with each style to determine which one you enjoy the most. The five types of soap making are:

- Cold process
- Hot process
- Melt and pour process
- Liquid soap making
- Re-batching or Hand Milled

The Cold Process

Keep in mind that in soap making, the cold process is the dragon level of all levels.

The game play becomes a little bit more complex, but don't worry we have got your back and we are here to guide you through it step by step. The reward here is that there are unlimited possibilities to how you can make your final product in terms of colours, shapes and natural additions. Moreover, you can 100% guarantee that your soap is home made from scratch.

Let us start with the basic ingredients you will need for making soap using the cold process.

- Lye flakes and clean distilled water
- A source of fat, whether animal fat or vegetable oil
- A natural soap dye of your choice, whether liquid or powder (optional but preferred)
- Soap pot along with other equipment which we will discuss in more details shortly
- Fragrance or an essential oil of your choice (optional but preferred)
- A mold of your desired shape
- A clean environment to work in and a cool dry place to let the soap cure in
- For aesthetics petals or exfoliates (optional)

How It Works

The essence of the cold soap making process is preparing lye and a source of fat and mixing it together.

1. Making The Lye Solution

The first step is to prepare the lye solution. For exact amounts, you will have to refer to your chosen recipe. Using your kitchen scale or digital scale, place the glass pitcher and set the scale to zero. Next you would be adding distilled water as per indicated in your recipe. Some recipes indicate weight; therefore you will place the pitcher on the scale. Other recipes indicate volume; therefore you can use your measuring cup.

Next it is time to measure up the lye.

Do so using your mason jar with a tight secure lid. Lye is an alkali and is dangerous to your skin. That is why you need to handle it using gloves and while wearing your safety goggles. If any lye flakes cling to your glove, remove them immediately. Place the Mason jar and its lid on the scale and set it to zero. Add in the lye flakes until the scale indicates the weight indicated in your chosen recipe.

You can replace the Mason jar with a plastic pitcher. However, don't use this pitcher for anything else except handling lye during your soap making process. After your weights are set as per indicated in your recipe, time to mix them up.

But be careful about this step. Take care to add the lye to the water bit by bit and not pour the water to the lye.

Gently start adding your lye flakes to the pitcher containing water. Add it bit by bit from a close but safe distance to avoid splashes. To dissolve the lye appropriately, stir the mixture gently and slowly, again without splashing. As the two react, you will start to hear fizzing sounds or feel heat which is normal. Don't let the solution touch your skin directly.

Keep your goggles and gloves on. Wash the item you used to stir with immediately after stirring. Don't forget to cover your pitcher containing your newly mixed lye water and let it settle for some time. Make sure it is tied securely and placed in a safe place away from pets or children. Caution should always be in mind around lye or lye water.

2. Preparing Oils

Get your handy scale again because we will weigh out your chosen oil as per the recipe, using the same method of adding the soap pot or a glass pitcher on the scale and setting it to zero. It is preferred to use the soap pot to weigh solid oils such as cocoa butter while using the glass pitcher for liquid oil such as olive oil. Slowly add the oil to your container till the scale hits the desired weight.

- **Examples of solid fat sources**

Cocoa butter, coconut or palm oil

- **Examples of liquid fat sources**

Castor oil, canola oil, olive oil, sunflower oil

If you are using a solid oil, melt it first using a sauce pan. This will shorten the step for you as you need to heat your chosen oil anyway. The oil needs to heat gradually, so apply medium heat and stir gently.

You need to watch the temperature of your oil using the thermometer and turn off the heat when it reaches about 110 F. However, you can't add it just yet to the lye water mixture. The oils temperature needs to drop to 100 F before it can be mixed with the lye water.

If you are using solid oil, make sure all the solid oil has come to a melt. If your recipe indicates a mixture of solid and liquid oils, add the liquid oils after all the solid fats melts. However, monitor your temperature again as this will lower the temperature of the overall oil mixture. Remember, you need it to be around 100 F when you mix it with the lye water.

3. Add Lye Water To The Oil Base

Once you mix these two, the saponification reaction will be instant, and the mixture will turn cloudy, indicating a chemical reaction where the lye and oil react in the presence of heat to make soap. The lye is no longer chemically lye that is why handmade soap is safe on the skin, it no longer contains lye as it all transformed to soap when it mixed with the hot oil.

Because from here on the process will happen quickly, you need to have your desired additions on standby, for example your fragrance bottles, essential oils, dye, spatulas, etc.

Gently add the lye mixture to the hot oil in the soap pot. You will notice a color change and that the mixture will start to be cloudy. Stir gently, preferably with a stick blender, although, keep it turned off at this point. After you have poured in all your lye water mixture, keep the glass pitcher that contained it in a safe spot for the time being until you safely clean it later. Right now, you need to stay with your new mixture.

If you are using a stick blender, turn it on now and let it mix the mixture in short bursts of a few seconds and repeat until you feel that both your lye water and oil have completely mixed until you reach trace. Trace is reached when the mixture has emulsified, meaning, when the mixture is left later, it will keep getting thicker and thicker with time as part of the process.

How To Know If You Have Reached Trace Point?

The stick blender has severely quickened the process of saponification and reaching trace takes seconds compared to hours using regular stirring.

If your mixture still has glistening oily liquidly floating between strokes, then all the oil has not mixed completely with your lye water yet. You will reach trace when the creamy consistency starts to slightly thicken and has a uniform consistency instead of having both thick and oily consistencies.

Why Is It Important To Reach Trace Point?

For many reasons, chief among them is that since tracing point is the point where all the mixture has emulsified and became soap particles instead of oil and lye, that means pouring the mixture before achieving trace results in having incomplete soap. This will lead to deformed soap or incompletely formed soap. Moreover, you will still have lye particles in your soap which will be very harmful to your skin. Therefore, you need to keep stirring until you have a think cake-like batter consistency with no glistening oil streaks. This mixture will also be easy to pour into a mold and will be of uniform consistency, you won't find oil dripping from the batter

It is safe to add your dye and fragrance in the light trace step before the thick medium trace step begins. Medium trace has a thicker consistency than light trace, resembling that of a pudding consistency.

You can test for it by trickling some of the batter from the blender and it will form visible soap streaks on the mixture's surface the way chocolate streaks on a cake. This is the most suitable time to add your natural hard additives such as leaves, exfoliate, petals, etc.

The final trace consistency is that which resembles a thick pudding batter. That is the trace consistency that will conform to its shape when poured into a mold and that is what you want. To reach this trace stage, you need to keep stirring with the stick blender. If you want to create soap frosting, you will need to extremely thicken your trace to get soap consistency for frosting or decorative purposes.

Keep in mind a very important false trace sign. When you use a solid trace, if it has not been thoroughly melted and heating, it can easily cool during the mixing process and give the false sensation of hardening mixture while in fact it is not hardening due to saponification but it is due to hardening of the solid fat. For that reason, make sure to adequately heat it.

Factors That Can Affect Trace Consistency

There is no doubt that using a stick will make you reach a medium and thick consistency trace faster than stirring by hand. If you would like to give your dye and fragrance some time to mix, consider stirring by hand using a spatula when you reach thin trace consistency.

Some fragrances and additives such as clay speed up the trace process and make your mixture thicken fast. Be mindful about such additions and the timing and method of stirring. It is preferred to switch to manual stirring after adding a fragrance.

The Hot Process

This process is like the cold process but involves using heat pots and "cooking" the soap rather than doing it cold. More detailed instructions can be found in the hot process recipes in the second part of this book.

The Melt and Pour Method

This is one of the easiest soap making processes and saves quite a lot of time.

In this process, you can use a premade soap base that has undergone the saponification process rather than spend time mixing fats with an alkali such as lye, which can be time consuming as it requires more preparation time. A readymade soap base contains glycerin and fatty acids as well as other natural Ingredients.

The melt and pour method is the perfect choice if you are a beginner, still exploring the arena and would like to play it safe.

All you have to do is purchase pre-made solid soap base instead of making it from scratch and you are ready to use the soap once it hardens, no unnecessary waiting for a cure time to pass such as with cold process.

How does this method work?

Head to a nearby arts and crafts store and look for a premade soap base. One of the best options to purchase are the clear glycerin or white premade soap bases. Don't use a bar of soap for this as it is not the same thing and will give you trouble while melting.

The next step would be to melt your solid premade soap base. To speed up this process, use a sharpened knife to cut the bar into small 1-inch chunks. Don't worry about exact measurements here. The goal is to have smaller pieces rather than one large chunk as smaller pieces will melt faster.

In a microwave, add your cut chunks in a microwave friendly dish and heat for 30 seconds. Take out the dish and stir your melted contents then reheat again for another 30 seconds then take out to stir again. Repeat this cycle of 30 seconds heat then stir until you feel the consistency of your melted soap base as completely liquid with no lumps or hard chunks in between. That is when your entire soap base has melted. Don't overheat it beyond that point.

Some people don't own a microwave in their house, it is possible to replace it with a saucepan filled with water to create a water bath. Heat the water and then put a glass bowl and let it float in the hot water. Put your soap base chunks in the glass bowl and watch it melt through the heat that transfers from the hot water to the glass bowl and consequently to the soap base chunks that melt eloquently. Don't forget to stir. Remove the bowl from the sauce pan when your soap base has completely melted and doesn't have any lumps.

Let your soap melt to cool down to around 50 degree Celsius. Do not add your essential oils or dye while the melt is still hot. Likewise, don't let it cool to the point of hardening. Add 2-3 drops of your desired dye depending on the colour intensity you desire. If you are using a powdered dye, dissolve 2-3 teaspoons of your powdered dye in some liquid glycerin as you can't add the power directly to your melt or else the colour will not get distributed evenly.

It is always wonderful to add a pleasant scent to your soap.

For 1 pound of soap, you can add 1 tablespoon of fragrance oil or half a tablespoon of essential oil. Make sure you use the ones labeled for soap making and not candle oils, to ensure they are friendly and soft on your skin.

Stir all your added dye and fragrance drops before the last step. The last step would be to pour your colored and fragranced melt into a mold of your choice then let it cool naturally for 12-24 hours. When your soap has completely solidified, take it out of the mold and it would be ready for use immediately. However, make sure the edges have dried completely.

The Liquid Soap Making Process

To make homemade liquid soap, we will have to use potassium hydroxide instead of sodium hydroxide. Sodium hydroxide makes hard soap, and potassium hydroxide makes liquid soap. Potassium hydroxide comes as flakes and not beads, and it is quite easier to dissolve than beads. After one knows how to make solid soap, the next thing to learn is how to make liquid soap. Liquid soap can be used as shampoo, body wash, or dish soap. It can also be used for washing clothes.

Equipment for making liquid soap:

- Crockpot
- Stick blender
- Potato masher
- Plastic spatula or stirrer
- Kitchen Scale - digital
- Gloves and goggles
- Plastic containers
- Thermometer

The Rebatching (Hand-Milling) Method

A similar quick and easy method is the rebatching method, also known as hand-milling. As the name suggests, it is often used to rebatch (make use of the soap you did) if there were any mistakes or if you didn't like the shape of the mold or messed it up during the design process.

You can also use this method if you want to get a taste of the soap making DIY experience without buying additional equipment. In that cause, you can use pre existing soap. However, readymade soap never melts easily, that is why, although you will heat it as we described in the melt and pour method, you will add few table spoons of water, glycerin, etc to soften up the mix, then with heat resistant gloves, you will add your soap melt in a Ziploc bag and knead it so make it into a mushy texture.

Similar to the melt and pour process, you can add the dye and fragrance to your mix in the rebatching method and then let it solidify. This will take 5-7 days however as you wait for all the water to evaporate. Don't get impatient and use the freezer. Rebatched soap does not have the most aesthetic look or feel, but it is a suitable solution to ruined soap or if you want to add your own colour and fragrance to existing soap.

Moreover, this method bypasses the drawback of adding stuff that get ruined by lye such as lavender buds that turn brown with lye. You can also use colours that are sensitive to the pH of lye that you can't use in the cold process. Similar is the case with being able to use light fragrances with the rebatching method which get masked when used in the cold process.

The benefits of both rebatching and melt and pour methods is that you don't have to deal with lye, which is feared by many people as it is a strong alkali. Moreover, you don't even need a lot of Ingredients to start with or complex calculations and you can immediately get to enjoying the soap once it solidifies. However, on the other hand, you have very little control over the raw Ingredients used as you are starting with something that someone else made, you don't control everything from scratch as with the cold method. If you would like to be the master of the experiment and totally in control of what goes in your soap, then the cold process is the best process for you.

Chapter 6: All About Oils And Fats

There are many oils and fats that can be used in the soap making process. In this section we will talk about the most common fats and oils used in soap making, their individual properties, and how they will enhance a bar of soap. The fats and oils used in soap making serve multiple purposes, including determining how much lather your soap produces, how hard your soap is, and how emollient or soothing the final product is.

- **Emollients**

These are the oils that are added to soap to increase the soap's moisturizing properties. Think of oils such as apricot, avocado, sweet almond, and jojoba, among others.

- **Lather-producing fats**

If you like a soap with a strong lather, coconut and castor oil are the two fats that produce the most lathering. More is not necessarily better with these two, and a little goes a long way in producing a heavy lather. Too much coconut oil can be overly cleansing, leading to dryness. Too much castor oil can make your soap dry and crumbly.

And, at a certain point, too much castor oil begins to take away the lathering property of a soap rather than contributing to it.

- **Hardeners**

Most hardeners are fats that are solid at room temperature. These fats help to solidify and harden your soap, extending its life. Examples include tallow (and other animal fats), vegetable shortening, and coconut oil. Olive oil doesn't act as a hardener on its own, but it can increase the hardening capacity of other oils.

There is an incredible variety of fats and oils to choose from when making soaps. When starting out, you will likely want to stick to the ones that you are familiar with, are reasonably affordable, and are easy to find. Following is a list of some of the best oils to consider for beginning and for advanced soap making.

- **Apricot Kernel Oil**

This very light oil is comparable to sweet almond oil and is well suited to sensitive skin types. It is rich in vitamins, has a very mild scent, and is absorbed readily into the skin.

- **Argan Oil**

Very rich in vitamin E and vitamin K. This oil is one of the more expensive oils that you will find on the market.

For this reason, it might be best to use Argan oil in rebatched, or hand milled soaps, so that you do not lose any large amount of the oil to the saponification process.

- **Avocado Seed Oil**

This oil is rich in vitamins A, E, and D. along with proteins and amino acids. It is a nice addition to add in soaps that you want to have a nice moisturizing property, especially since it is easily absorbed by the skin.

- **Babassu Oil**

While this oil is lesser known that many of the others that you will find on this list, it is worth mentioning because it is a good substitute for coconut oil in soaps that you want to produce a strong, lasting lather. Babassu oil tends to maintain moisture and be less drying that coconut oil can be when used in larger amounts.

- **Beeswax**

Beeswax, while not used often in soaps, is a nice additive to hand soaps because of the softening affect that it has on the skin. It is sometimes added to soaps as a thickener, aiding in the tracing process.

- **Canola Oil**

Canola oil is rich in essential fatty acids, and in some cases, it is blended with olive oil, making it a less expensive choice than pure olive oil.

It is a high oleic oil, which means that it will take longer trace. This is beneficial when you wish to make specialty soaps where techniques, such as swirling, demand that you have a longer time to work with the soap.

- **Castor Oil**

This oil is another of the main lather producing oils, when used in a proportion of five to ten percent. It acts as a humectant when added to other oils and is a good choice for super fatted soaps.

- **Cocoa Butter**

Will add a hardening component to your soap recipes. In the final product, cocoa butter provides a barrier on the skin that helps to preserve and maintain moisture. Some people find the scent of cocoa butter overpowering or displeasing. Unscented cocoa butter is available for soap making purposes:

- **Coconut Oil**

One of the best oils to use to produce a hard, long lasting soap. It is top of class in lathering and cleansing capabilities. The only downside of coconut oil is that when used to high of a proportion can be potentially drying to some people's skin.

- **Hazelnut Oil**

Similar to sweet almond oil in properties, this oil is light and readily absorbed into your skin. Often used in massage oils, this is a nice, easily absorbed oil to add to your soaps and can replace olive oil in most formulas, if adjustments are made for the hardening properties of olive oil.

- **Hemp Oil**

One of the most healing oils that you can add to your soap, hemp or hemp seed oil is an excellent choice for soaps that are crafted for dry skin, aging skin or damaged skin that needs extra care.

- **Jojoba Oil**

Jojoba is a light oil that is an excellent conditioner. It can be a little more expensive than other oils, however, using jojoba as a complimentary oil or in supper fatting will provide enough of the oil to receive its many benefits.

- **Lard**

This is one of the least expensive resources that you can use to create high quality soaps. Lard produces a good, rich later and contributes hardening properties as well. The scent is mellow in the finished product and undetectable if any other scenting agents are used in the soap.

- **Olive Oil**

This is one of the most well know oils for soap making. A pure olive oil soap is creamy and luxurious. Most of the time however, olive oil is used in combination with other oils to produce rich, moisturizing soaps. You can purchase olive oil as a food grade oil or as a therapeutic grade oil. You will notice slight differences in color and aroma of the olive oil depending upon which you choose.

Keep in mind that many food grade olive oils are cut with other oils, so if you purchase straight off of your grocer's shelves make sure that the product you are getting is one hundred percent pure and from a reputable supplier.

It is ok to use an olive oil that has another oil added to it, just keep in mind that the saponification values of the two (or more) oils might be different and adjustments might need to be made in the amount of lye typically used for olive oil. You can also purchase therapeutic grade olive oil and olive oil directly from craft and soap suppliers.

- **Palm Oil**

Another readily available oil, palm or vegetable oil is found in most kitchen pantries. Again, if you purchase this oil directly from your grocery store, make sure that you are aware of what the contents of the oil really are. Palm oil is light in color and scent, and makes a nice, neutral choice for an oil.

- **Shea Butter**

This thick, rich butter is known for retaining moisture and can be used in place of cocoa butter, which has a heavier scent that some people view as unpleasant. Shea butter is excellent to use in facial and hair care bars.

- **Sweet Almond Oil**

This oil is rich in vitamins and minerals. It is also very light in scent, which makes it an excellent addition to soaps that are created to be unscented and moisturizing. It is rich in protein and absorbs easily into the skin.

- **Tallow**

There seem to be two separate schools of thought concerning soaps that use animal fats. People either love them or do not like the idea of animal products in their soaps and stay away. Beef tallow makes a hard, but very mild and moisturizing soap.

Tallow is readily available from most meat counters or butchers' shops, but will need to be rendered before use, but can be purchase in an already rendered form from some suppliers.

Something to keep in mind, if you are a little apprehensive about using animal fats in your soap: by using tallow in your soaps, you are helping to use all the parts of an animal, including the fats which would only end up in a landfill if another use is not found for them.

Contrary to common perception, the use of animal fats can actually be environmentally friendly.

- **Vegetable Shortening**

This is a good alternative to palm oil and as a substitution for animal fats. Vegetable shortening has a hardening component to it and produces a bar of soap that is mild and conditioning. Vegetable shortening is readily available from your grocery store, just make sure that what you purchase is pure vegetable oil without any additives.

- **Wheat Germ Oil**

This oil is rich in vitamins, especially vitamins A, D and E. This oil is very nourishing to the skin. It is slightly thicker than the lighter oils of this list and has a very mild and slightly nutty scent to it. Makes a nice addition to beauty bars.

Chapter 7: Herbs & Other Natural Additives

Enriching Your Soap

- **Milk**

Milk makes soap very creamy. It can however be very tricky to use milk in soap. Due to the intense and sustained heat of the chemical reaction of the lye, the proteins and fats in the milk burn and the milk can turn a dark yellow or orange color. Because of this you may have problems getting your soap to trace and your soap can even smell burnt or like sour milk. There are still options if you want to add milk, you can freeze the milk until it is slushy and then slowly add the lye. You can also add milk after trace. You can use liquid milk or powdered milk. If you use powdered milk, dissolve it in a small amount of water or oil, to make it easier to incorporate into the soap.

- **Coffee, Tea and Juice**

Coffee, Tea and Juice can be used in your soap making imparting their color and aroma.

Depending on the type of soap you want to make, you can use these liquids in the lye solution or add them in concentrated or powdered forms at trace.

- **Honey**

Honey has amazing humectant and antimicrobial properties making it a wonderful ingredient for soap. Add honey at trace, mixing well to combine.

- **Exfoliants**

Exfoliants can be added to soap at trace. How much and which type of exfoliant depends on the purpose of the soap. An oatmeal face soap will have a small amount of very finely ground oatmeal, where a hand soap for gardeners may include quite a lot of cornmeal. You can add many different types of exfoliants to your soap: Ground spices, dried herbs and flowers, ground nuts, seeds or flowers. Add exfoliants at trace so they stay evenly suspended throughout the soap.

- **Botanicals**

Botanicals make lovely additions to soap and lend texture, visual appeal and aroma. Add them at trace. Some common botanicals you can use include lavender, chamomile, rose petals, citrus peel, parsley, green tea & mint.

- **Vitamins and Skin Nutrients**

Vitamins and Skin Nutrients help the skin to stay healthy and fight the effects of aging. Vitamins and Skin Nutrients that you can add at trace include: Vitamins A, C & E, B-Vitamins or B-Complex, Selenium, and Biotin. You can buy these in liquid form or grind up tablets.

Scenting Your Soap

To perfume homemade soap, there are a lot of fragrances that can be purchased online or from your local grocery store. The following are fragrances that can be used for soaps that are homemade.

Vanilla, coconut, peppermint, rose, sandalwood, orange, lemon, chocolate, honey, Jasmine dream, cherry blossom, apricot, apple, apple pie, argan, cinnamon, lavender, cacao, mango, acai berry, applejack and peel, apple berry spice, banana raspberry, black raspberry banana, black cherry, cinnamon and cloves, Egyptian musk, grapefruit citrus, Japanese cherry blossom, jasmine, lilac, lemongrass, orange fresh, orange peel, pineapple express, sweet peaches, tangerine vanilla, vanilla butter, wintergreen, and warm apple pie.

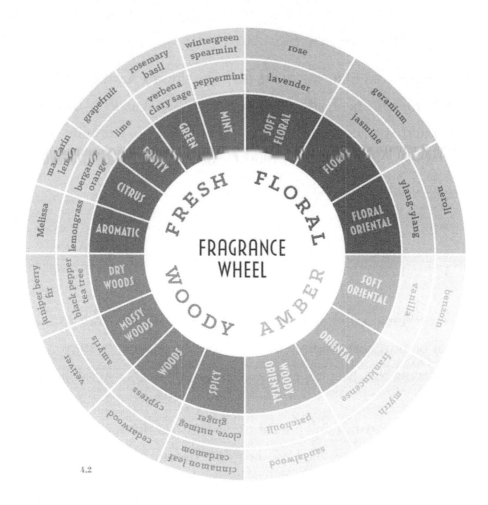

FRAGRANCE WHEEL

FRESH · FLORAL · WOODY · AMBER

wintergreen spearmint · rose · rosemary basil · lavender · geranium · grapefruit · verbena clary sage · peppermint · jasmine · lime · MINT · SOFT FLORAL · GREEN · FLORAL · mandarin lemon · FRUITY · ylang-ylang · bergamot orange · CITRUS · neroli · Melissa · AROMATIC · FLORAL ORIENTAL · lemongrass · juniper berry fir · DRY WOODS · SOFT ORIENTAL · black pepper tea tree · vanilla · benzoin · MOSSY WOODS · WOODY ORIENTAL · ORIENTAL · frankincense · vetiver · amyris · WOODS · SPICY · myrrh · cypress · clove, nutmeg ginger · patchouli · cedarwood · cardamom cinnamon leaf · sandalwood

4.2

The list is endless. You can order any fragrance of your choice online to use for your homemade soap.

Coloring Your Soap

Homemade soap, when finished without color, is translucent and almost transparent when cured.

But if you wish to add color, you can use natural colors, but don't forget that they fade easily because of atmospheric oxygen and the lye in the soap, which is able to change the color of the soap depending on the pH of the soap.

Artificial colors are quite potent. It is important that you use them in very small quantities. Use different types of colors for different types of soap processes.

Pigments

Pigments are useful for colored cold processed soap. You can use up to five different types of colors in the soap, depending on your designing skill. It can also be used for melt and pour processed soap. The only disadvantage is that they can clump or speckle the soap. To overcome this, always dissolve the color in glycerin or isopropyl alcohol before adding it to the soap. There are plenty to choose from and brightly colored ones too.

Examples of pigments are:

- Green chromic oxide pigment
- Activated charcoal
- Dried lavender
- Lagoon green jojoba
- Ocean blue jojoba

Micas

Micas are minerals that are shining substances which come in many different colors and are coated with other colorants called F & D colorants, pigments or a combination of them to get different colors. This is very good for the melt and pour process of making homemade soap. Micas come in a variety of colors. You should use them with care and read the instructions carefully that come along with the colors before using them for cold process soap production. Nevertheless, they can be used to design or decorate the top of the soap. Examples are:

- Blue mica
- Cellini red mica
- Shamrock green mica
- Yellow lip mica
- Snowflakes sparkle mica
- Kings gold mica
- Party pink mica
- Desert red mica
- Rose gold mica

While mica produces beautiful soaps with the melt and pour process, with soaps made by a cold process, it might disappear.

It could also turn into a different color in cold process soap production, although the outcome may still be fabulous. An example is amethyst purple mica that changes from purple to fabulous lovely yellow color in cold process soap production.

- **How to Use Mica**

Dissolve 1 teaspoonful of mica into 1 tablespoonful of isopropyl alcohol and add to the melted soap base. Usage should be 1/2 teaspoonful for a 1-pound weight of soap made using the melt and pour process, while for the cold process you need 1/16 of a teaspoonful per pound weight of soap. For hot process soap, use a 1/4 teaspoonful of mica per pound weight of soap.

Lab Colors

These are liquid dyes which are very concentrated and are useful both for cold process and melt and pour process soaps. These dyes need to be diluted before you use them. There are varieties of them, and they are reliable long-lasting water-based colors of high quality. They are the most reliable to use for any soap made from any of the different processes.

Examples of lab colors:

- Blue nature tint

- Caramel nature tint
- Green nature tint
- Lemon yellow nature tint
- Pink nature tint
- Red nature tint
- Violet nature tint
- Orange nature tint
- Azure blue
- Canary
- Cimmeron
- Citrus green
- Java beans

Recommended concentration for soap: 8-10 ml of diluted lab color for 1 pound of soap.

Natural Colorants

They too create beautiful colors in the melt and pour process produced soap and cold process produced soap, but they are less bright when compared with lab colors. This disadvantage can be overcome by using two or more of the natural colorants to create a sharper color.

Titanium oxide can be used to lighten some colors of soap which may be produced as a result of using particular oils in case we want a color different from the color imposed by the oil on the soap.

Natural colorants can even be found in your kitchen or your grocery store. You can also order them online.

Examples of natural colors:

- Activated charcoal - black.
- Alfalfa - green.
- Alkanet - purple.
- Beetroot - pink to dull brown pink.
- Bentonite - off white.
- Black walnut - purple-brown.
- Carrot - yellow to orange.
- Chlorophyll - green.
- Cloves - brown.
- Cocoa powder - brown.
- Coffee ground - black to brown.

- Cucumber - pale green.

- Spinach - light green.

- Turmeric - golden brown to amber.

NATURAL ADDITIVE	WHEN TO USE	COLOR	AMOUNT PER POUND OF SOAP
Activated Charcoal	Trace	Gray/Black	1–1½ teaspoons
Ground Cinnamon	Trace	Brown	2 teaspoons
Brewed Coffee	Cooled and used in place of some water before adding lye; used grounds added later	Brown	2 teaspoons
Cocoa Powder	Trace	Brown	1 tablespoon
Ground Cloves	Hot Oil Infusion	Brown	½ ounce in place of olive oil in recipe
Spirulina Powder	Trace or Lye Water	Green	½–1 teaspoon
Parsley	Oil Infusion	Green	½ ounce in place of olive oil in recipe
Liquid Chlorophyll	Trace	Green	½–1 teaspoon
Alfalfa	Oil Infusion	Green	½ ounce in place of olive oil in recipe
Burdock Leaf	Oil Infusion	Green	½ ounce in place of olive oil in recipe
Comfrey Leaf	Oil Infusion	Green	½ ounce in place of olive oil in recipe
Dandelion Leaf	Oil Infusion	Green	½ ounce in place of olive oil in recipe
Ground Calendula Flowers	Lye Water	Yellow	¼ cup
Ground Turmeric	Oil Infusion	Yellow	½ ounce in place of olive oil in recipe

NATURAL ADDITIVE	WHEN TO USE	COLOR	AMOUNT PER POUND OF SOAP
Annatto seeds	Oil Infusion	Yellow	2 ounces for orange, ½–1 ounce for yellow in place of olive oil
Ground Ginger	Oil Infusion	Cream/Yellow	1 ounce in place of olive oil in recipe
Safflower Powder	Oil Infusion	Yellow	½ ounce in place of olive oil in recipe
Moroccan Orange Clay	Trace	Tan/Orange	1–2 teaspoons
Saffron	Oil Infusion	Yellow/Orange	½ ounce in place of olive oil in recipe
Paprika	Trace or Lye Water	Orange	1–2 teaspoons
Tomato Purée	Trace	Dark Orange	¼ cup—decrease water for amount of purée added
Pumpkin Purée	Trace	Orange	¼ cup—decrease water for amount of purée added
Carrot Juice	Trace	Orange	¼ cup—decrease water for amount of purée added
Rose Clay	Trace or Lye Water	Pink	2 teaspoons
Madder Root Powder	Trace or Lye Water	Pink/Red	2–3 teaspoons
Alkanet Root Powder	Trace or Oil Infusion	Purple	1 teaspoon or ½ ounce oil infusion in place of olive oil in recipe
Black Walnut Hull Powder	Lye Water	Brown/Purple	2 teaspoons
Indigo Powder	Lye Water	Deep Blue	½–1 teaspoon
Woad Powder	Oil Infusion	Sky Blue	½ ounce in place of olive oil in recipe

These colors can be extracted from their dried compounds and macerated in distilled water to extract the color. This extraction is what will now serve as the distilled water.

After extraction, the distilled water will become colored with the compound, and then the liquid is filtered with a sieve to remove unwanted materials.

The filtered liquid is now used to dissolve the lye. How do you get the color out of the compound?

Weigh out the quantity of the dried natural compound and then pour in the distilled water measured out to dissolve the lye.

Following this, boil the combination. Boiling will hasten the maceration and extraction of the coloring material into the liquid which will make the procedure faster.

After using the wire cutter to cut your soap log into smaller units, you can now use a specific soap mold to get the shape you want.

After getting maybe an inch-thick slice of soap from your soap bar or log you can you use, for example, a heart-shaped or a square-shaped mold and press it into the slice you cut earlier to get a specific shape you want.

Another beautiful thing about hand-crafted soaps is the beautiful shapes you can choose from. You can use a heart-shaped mold, or you can even have multiple colors in your soap.

Soap making is an art and also a science, so the variables are endless. If you are creative, you can get myriads of designs just using your innovations and ingenuity.

Chapter 8: Scenting and Coloring your Homemade Soap in a Natural Way

If you have already started to prepare the soap at home in a basic, uncolored and unscented version, you may have the desire to take it to the next level to obtain aromatic soaps with pleasant nuances. The most immediate way to color your homemade soap is to use food coloring agents, but there are much more natural alternatives.

To color and perfume soap without using artificial colors or synthetic fragrances is to turn to the world of plants, spices and minerals, as well as essential oils. The main trick is to add the most delicate coloring and scenting Ingredients, such as essential oils and spices, only in the final part of the soap preparation, when the process is at the ribbon stage: the soap, while being blended, takes on the typical consistency of custard, and if a drop is dropped on a solid surface, it manages to leave a trace. Oleolites, decoctions and infusions are used, instead, already at the beginning of the preparation. Here are some tips to perfume and color the soap in a natural way.

Essential Oils

The essential oils are extracted from flowers, aromatic plants, bark and citrus peel. They are very concentrated and fragrant. Therefore, small quantities will be enough to perfume homemade soap. The essential oils must be added at the ribbon stage, so that the action of the soda does not eliminate their scent. It is possible to fix the scent of the essential oils so that they last longer, mixing them with a small amount of corn or rice starch to pour into the soap. Or it is advisable to have them absorbed by the dried herbs that will eventually be used to prepare the soap.

Dried Herbs And Flowers

Dried herbs and flowers help to decorate and perfume the soap at the same time. These are precious Ingredients that are always added at the ribbon stage. Among the most fragrant flowers, to be used in the dried version to decorate and perfume, we find lavender and chamomile, of which petals and flower heads should be kept. Among the most perfumed herbs are sage and rosemary. As for the color, you can use ground dried mint to obtain shades of green and ground dried marigold for yellow. If you want to decorate the surface of the soap with dried herbs or dried flowers, place them on the bottom of the mound before pouring it.

Oxides And Mica

Oxides and mica, both powdered Ingredients, are coloring substances of mineral origin. They can be purchased in natural cosmetics shops and offer products for making DIY cosmetics. They can be found mainly online. They are added at the ribbon stage. The advice is to pour them little by little, e.g. one teaspoon tip at a time, in order to obtain the desired shades.

Infusions And Decoctions

Unlike the other Ingredients, infusions and decoctions should not be added at the moment of the tape phase, but at the beginning of the preparation of the soap, in place of the amount of water indicated by the recipe you have decided to follow. The infusions and decoctions of flowers or herbs should be filtered very carefully through a strainer. The quantity of herbs to be used varies according to the color or intensity of the perfume you will want to give the soap. Usually you will get subtle scents and nuances. Decoctions and infusions of sage, chamomile, rosemary and lavender are the most suitable. For example, the decoction of sage gives the soap a golden yellow color.

Cocoa And Coffee

Cocoa and coffee, both in powder form, are useful for both coloring and perfuming soap. You will obtain a coloring with shades of brown. The scent of cocoa, in particular, is very persistent. Add the cocoa and coffee powder little by little in the ribbon phase, until you get the desired shade. The coffee beans can be placed on the bottom of the mound to decorate the soap.

Oleolites

Oleolites or oily macerates prepared with flowers and aromatic herbs give the soap colored shades, fragrance and healing properties. They can be replaced in whole or in part to the quantity of oil indicated in the recipe that you will follow for the preparation of the soap. Remember to always calculate the amount of oil, water and soda to use based on the tables online. One of the most effective oil macerates to color the soap is the St. John's wort oleolite prepared with olive oil, which takes on the characteristic red color. It is also possible to prepare oleolites of flowers, such as lavender, calendula or chamomile, and herbs, such as rosemary or sage. Fresh flowers and herbs are normally used, to be left to macerate in a jar filled with olive oil for 15 to 30 days.

Spices

Among the Ingredients useful for coloring the soap in a natural way cannot miss the spices. They must be used in powder form and added during the preparation of the soap at the ribbon stage. Among the spices that guarantee the most evident colors are turmeric, saffron, curry and paprika. Cinnamon is excellent for perfuming, as well as for obtaining rosy shades.

Herbs Dyeworks

The same dyeing herbs that are used for natural hair or fabric coloring can also be useful for soap decoration. They are used in powder form and added little by little in the ribbon phase. Among the most common dyeing herbs are henna, which is useful for obtaining an orange color, indigo, which is dyed purple-blue, walnut husk for brown and alkane for red. They can be purchased, already in powder form, online or in herbalist's shops.

Vegetables

Some vegetable fruits have strong coloring properties and can be used to dye soap.

The coloring effect is due to their pigment and beta-carotene content. In particular, to obtain orange-yellow soaps it is possible to use carrot juice, to be used alone instead of water or in combination with the amount of water indicated in the recipe.

You can experiment with fruit and vegetable juices to obtain soaps with different shades. Sugar-free juices should be used, preferably prepared at home. With spinach juice, for example, you will get shades of green.

Clays

The clays are useful to give more or less intense shades to the soap and to obtain exfoliating soaps. They are used in powder and added to the soap in the ribbon phase little by little, depending on the desired effect. The most suitable products for soap coloring are pink clay and green clay. Natural clays can be purchased online or in an herbalist's shop.

Chapter 9: Decorating Your Homemade Soaps

Decorating Your Finished Product

One of the best finishing touches that can be given to your natural homemade soap is to decorate them with beautiful designs, most especially if you have the plans of giving them out as a gift or selling them. Adding decorations will add finesse and a fresh touch of sophistication to the homemade soap bars. You can easily decorate the homemade soap bars with simple things such as magazines to pictures to beautiful dried herbs or flowers. The list is endless.

Environment-Friendly Soap Packaging Concepts

You can use simple eco-friendly soap packaging concepts to pack your natural homemade soaps. All these concepts are quite simple and relatively cheap since the materials to be used for the packaging includes everyday materials such as lace, paper, fabric, string, and other natural materials.

Since the homemade soaps are good for the skin, it will not be a bad idea of you gift wrap some and give them out as presents. If you are thinking what I am thinking, there will be quite a number of homemade soaps and scrub bars on the gift list. Making homemade gifts can be used as a pastime, save you extra cash, and it can make giving out gifts more personal. If you handle it properly, producing a few extra soap bars when making your personal soap and decorating the soap bars with cute materials is a brilliant way to go about it. These homemade soaps can be given out with a small card, place in a small hamper, or you can tuck it inside Christmas stockings. These are some of the simple ideas you can use to make your homemade soap a standout gift. I like to make use of things that look good and natural, both in feel and make. All of these simple concepts of gift wrapping your own homemade soap can be remade in the comfort of your house with bits of string and paper that you have already. The rest can be easily sourced from the nearest craft store.

Simple Soap Wrapping With Bows

One of the simplest ways of decorating homemade soap is by using a bow. All sorts of materials can be used to make a simple bow.

Materials that include plain string, raffia ribbon, cooking twine, bakers' twine, you can even use an embroidery thread.

Use what you have in your house already, or you can visit the local craft store to get more variety.

One thing I will advise is that you should go with strings colors that contrast the color of the soap. For instance, if the color of your soap is all white and creamy, then you should opt for a colorful material like a red string to make the bow.

With soaps that are colored, pick a material with a natural tone, a raffia ribbon, for example. Even the soap that is the most rustic will look pretty with a bow to doll up. Taking this concept up a notch, I will recommend that you place three or four small bars of soap with different scents or shades in the same box. Now imagine how cute this will be, each soap properly dressed in its own special bow.

Decorate Homemade Soap With Lace

Another excellent and simple idea that can be used to package a homemade soap is by decorating it with lace. Just cut out enough lace that will wrap around the soap comfortably and then put the soap bars in the gift box. Different colors and patterns will sit pretty on the soaps when they are placed beside each other. These will look really good as a gift alongside other vintage gifts like a teacup candle.

You can easily source for the lace from the nearest fabric store, or you can purchase it over the internet. I will recommend that you stay away from vintage lace because they cost quite a fortune. Another bonus of using modern and cheaper lace is that it is made of acrylic materials as such it will not take in much moisture as opposed to old fashioned lace that absorbs moisture.

Although several laces come in narrow ribbons, it is possible to source for broader types, and these wider types can cover almost all the bar in one single wrap thus the final decoration is usually really beautiful. When it comes to packaging, decorating and gifting soap, using decorations that contrast each other can actually add more elegance to the homemade soap bar.

Packaging Soap With Paper

If your homemade soap is properly cured, it is okay to wrap the homemade soap bars in a paper. You can use a gift-wrapping paper, brown parchment paper, handmade paper, tissue paper, or even baking paper. Packaging and wrapping homemade soap bars in the paper makes each bar of soap look like a mini- gift. Basically, any type of paper can be used.

Imagine a soft brown paper wrapped around a soap bar, finish the decoration with a sprig of evergreen leaves and natural twine. The brown paper here is a translucent grease-proof paper, and this sort of paper goes by the market name of wax paper, and it usually comes in white, brown and other bright colors.

During the holidays, you might find this wax paper in festive patterns. What makes this soap wrapping type exceptional is that you can tuck in some dried flowers and use those to add a more natural tone to the decoration. However, you must remember that tape will not stick to some wax papers if you find yourself in this situation, tie a string around it to keep it in place.

Decorate Homemade Soap With Herbs And Flowers

It does not have to be just papers and ribbons when it comes to decorating and packing homemade soap bars.

You can make use of both fresh and dried flowers and foliage to give your soap bar more attention. This can be achieved in more than one way and if you are going with the fresh material you have to be more careful. First of all, it is possible for you to decorate homemade soap bars with herbs or flowers during the process of making the soap.

When the soap is fully mixed and has reached trace, the soap should be poured in the mold. The herbs or flower can be placed on top of the soap; thus, the flower or herb will solidify and cure with the soap.

In a situation like this, the soap itself is the packaging and can be presented as a gift the way it is, or you can tie a simple bow around it. One simple decoration for homemade soap is the simple recipe of using fresh cedar leaves to make a natural leaf etching on homemade soap bars.

Packaging Handmade Soap With Greenery

Another method of decorating your soap is by tying dried or greenery herbs around your soap bar like a bow. You can use a few stems of dried sage, dried lavender, with the soap bar plus a washcloth decoration, or a sprig of holly. If you are using new greenery, make sure that the soap bar is decorated on the day you are planning to give them out as gifts.

Failure to do this on D-day will make the fresh plant wither and dampen the soap bar and every other material that was used to pack it, thus creating a mess.

To use dried flowers – simply melt a little amount of paraffin wax, then use a pastry brush to apply it to the natural homemade soap bar.

Add the dried flower immediately, so it becomes glued to the soap.

To add pictures or designs to your soap – use a decoupage adhesive to achieve this aim. Brush it slightly on the bar soap and then append the picture quickly. Also, have it in mind to add a small amount of the adhesive to the picture as well.

It is advisable to measure everything before you start the decorative process, in bids to ensure that the picture fits perfectly on the bar of soap. Once you have glued the picture to the soap bar, then brush the picture with adhesive and give it time to dry. Keep repeating this process until there is like 3 to 5 coats on the picture.

Packaging Soap With Other Beauty Items

One interesting thing about making your own personal homemade soap bar is the ability to create items that match each other.

Peppermint lip balm goes in tandem with peppermint soap, while lavender soap bar goes hand in hand with lavender body balm.

Place these items side by side in a paper box, tie a pretty ribbon around the box in the form of a bow, and voila — homemade gifts that relatively cost you nothing.

Honeycomb Soap

This decorative effect is one of the easily decoration and soap designs that you can add to your bar soap! Make sure you keep a scrap of bubble wrap the next time you receive one in a shipping parcel. The smaller bubble wrap between 3/16" to ¼" produces the best result. Cut the bubble wrap to size, in such a way that it fits the base of the mold. Place the bubble wrap on the already lined mold and ensure the bubble wrap is facing up. Gently pour the soap onto the bubble wrap and wait 24 hours or more for the soap to set properly. Once this is achieved, remove the soap from the mold and peel off the bubble wrap from the bottom of the soap bar. The base of the soap bar will have a simple design that resembles a honeycomb. And it looks great!

The sky is the starting point when it comes to producing and decorating homemade soap bars. The ideas giving in this chapter are the tip of an iceberg because I am quite sure you several more are already popping up in your head.

Some of these packaging and decorating ideas are all-natural and cost relatively nothing, and all would make cute and presentable homemade gifts.

Make Homemade Soap For Gifts

I think by now you should be able to make your own homemade soap, if not, take your time to read the process earlier explained in this book, and I am sure you will have it figured out.

Chapter 10: Starting Your Soap Making Business

Take a deep breath. Slow down. By the time you have made your first loaf of soap you are probably already putting a beautiful craft table together in your imagination for customers to fuss over. Setting your fresh cut pieces up on the kitchen counter gets your thoughts moving about how realistic it is creating something someone would love to buy. Of course, where are these people? How do I get to them and show off my product?

Don't rush. You have a bit of homework to do at this point. First, you have to make sure you are legal to sell your products and follow the rules about preparing your products before you can think about selling them. Makes sure your Ingredients are labeled properly. Now, you may be reading this from your kitchen table in any given state and each state may have different rules about how to set up your small business. Some states will have almost no rules, but you need to know what they are, so you don't sabotage your own efforts before you begin.

Today you can go online to your local government websites who will have this information readily available to you. You need to look into whether or not you need a reseller permit.

This is easy, it's no hassle to do this. Basically, this assigns you a tax id number when you report your sales to your local tax office. Don't for a minute think that by setting up a table at a craft fair and accepting cash this means that you should neglect having your small business set up properly. You are only protecting yourself from the beginning while establishing a credible business by filing as required.

This may seem like a no brainer to some, but there is one lady who comes to mind who did not do this. She was a regular at a Connecticut Farmers Market. Somehow her reseller information was never requested, and her table was a regular set up once a week. Her products were unique and extremely natural looking and smelled almost medicinal. After several months her table was popular enough for customers to come looking for her, and she was sure to sell out every time she set up her stand. This was great after the first year, but then a village store popped up in town with exactly the same name of her products. Lo and behold, her customers started to wander into the shop downtown. Once you have your reseller permit contact your city clerk and file a DBA (doing business as) document. This usually costs a dollar, and it declares your name. No one else in town will be allowed to file their DBA under this name as long as you are in existence.

How you use these suggestions will depend on what you have in mind when it comes to making a few dollars and your personality.

First, the most obvious way is to design a table for local craft fairs, flea markets, and trade shows. Start small. First think about your table. The first time I successfully sold my products at an outdoor event I made 10 loaves of soap and cut them up nicely. I spread them across a pretty table with handmade cards describing each recipe and clearly written prices. The cost of making 10 loaves of soap was about $100. After each piece was sold the total return was $400. You can make a table look beautiful and start your business with about $100 in product. (I did not use the cheapest materials. You can do this on the cheap if you sculpt your recipes, and many customers will be happy with your product.)

There are three types of outdoor events where you can regularly set up your stand. Flea markets, Farmers Markets, and Seasonal Fairs. Each one has a different personality and you can expect different customers. You may want to explore different set up environments to see how your customers will be different.

Outdoor events may be as easy as showing up at a vendor call time, or you may need to get approved through an application process. The first thing you need to do is use your Google powers and start looking up the places you know of first and email with your questions.

After a few inquiries you will start to get the same types of replies, and you will see the trends in barrier to entry.

Flea markets: big flea markets bring in deal hunters. Often, you will not need to be approved in advance to set your table up at a flea market. Sometimes you will, you must ask before you show up. Renting a flea market space at an outdoor event will get you outdoors on a sunny weekend and mingling with people. There price to rent a space will typically cost you anywhere between 25 – 50 dollars.

You can expect to park your car that you have packed in your rented space and set your tent or table up in a neat row next to your neighbor for the customers to browse. Flea markets include antiques, second hand stuff, and in some cases the guy who just cleaned out his garage and offers everything up for a few dollars. Your customers may vary.

In New England we have flea markets that will bring out thousands and thousands of people. You can do very well with your products, but you may discover some flea markets are like a giant yard sale where people expect everything to be sold for a dollar. In your area, go online and find two or three of the largest flea markets closest to you. Visit them and get an idea of what you're walking into.

Farmers Markets: Farmers markets are a different animal completely. Depending on where you are located, they may not bring out as many people, but you will find a customer who has an appreciation for exactly the thing you bring.

Farmers markets bring people who want natural nutrients and chemical free products.

In today's commercial soap and shampoo, you have to go out of your way to read the packaging on a soap label to find products that are detergent or chemical free. Your products are exactly that, and pretty to look at, and typically sold at a similar price for anything in the store.

A farmer's market will have guidelines and rules about the product you sell. Since you are not selling food, your guidelines are much easier. You will need to get approval before joining a farmer's market, but many do not require you to pay to rent a space, so this is a benefit compared to a flea market. A farmer's market is usually held on public property such as a wide street or a town green, where a flea market is usually private property owned by a private company to which the company gives the public access.

The third way to sell your products is online. In today's world, you are only helping yourself by becoming computer savvy and create an online presence for yourself. This will allow more people to find you, and you can even make sales online.

Selling at your local markets and online complement each other very nicely. Online customers will have consumer confidence when they know that you are a real live person who is happy to meet face to face. This is making online people who are sitting far away feel that your product is real and genuine.

 Also, if you have a customer who has found you at your outdoor event but is just traveling through you may have a future internet customer if they wish to buy from you again.

Selling online isn't work free. It isn't passive, and it certainly isn't any sort of get rich quick scheme. Once you have decided to put the effort into marketing yourself and selling your products online you quickly discover that there is a real learning curve to all this work, but the great part is, you can do it. At the end of the day, it's all about what you're willing to put into it.

First, create your Facebook business page. If you do nothing else, you don't need to sell any items on Facebook, just offer a little communication, and updates as you see fit. If people who have found your craft table think to look you up on Facebook, you will stay in their memory the next time they stop by your market. This little memory can create a fond association and bring your customers back to you.

If you hate computers, dive into your digital fears by making this little page. In no time it will become second nature and you will get a little delight in seeing local people like your page.

PART II: HOMEMADE SOAP RECIPES

Chapter 11: Cold Process Soap Recipes

Safflower And Ginger Soap Cold Process

Ingredients

- Babassu Oil- 12.8 oz.
- Coconut Oil- 10.2 oz.
- Olive Oil- 15.3 oz.
- Shea Butter- 2.6 oz.
- Sunflower Oil- 10.2 oz.
- Sodium Hydroxide Lye- 7.4 oz.
- Distilled Water- 15.2 oz.- 1 oz.
- Ginger Essential Oil
- Yellow Brazilian Clay
- Titanium Dioxide
- Safflower Powder
- Poppy Seeds
- Safflower Petals

Instructions:

1. Start by slowly mixing the 7.4 ounces of lye with 15.3 ounces of distilled water. Allow them to cool down to below 100°F.

2. Take out a pan and melt your Babassu Oil, Coconut Oil, Olive Oil, Shea Butter, Sunflower Oil. Don't overheat the oils. Whisk until they are mixed well.

3. Use a thermometer to check the temperature of the oil mixture. Ensure that it is 100°F above the lye solution.

4. While you wait for it to get to the right temperature, mix your Yellow Brazilian Clay and Titanium Dioxide in a bowl. Whisk well.

5. Once the temperatures are right, mix the lye-water with the oil mixture before you add your whisked Yellow Brazilian Clay and Titanium Dioxide mixture.

6. Hand-mix it before you use a stick blender to mix it well.

7. After that, add your Ginger Essential Oil.

8. Put the mixture in the pre-lined mold then spray with 99% isopropyl alcohol to prevent soda ash.

9. Press your poppy seeds and safflower petals on the soap bars.

10. Refrigerate them for about two days.

11. Immediately after your soap has hardened, remove it from your mold, then cut it.

12. Allow it to cure for at least 4 weeks.

Beet Cold Process Soap

Ingredients:

- Babassu Oil 1.7 oz.
- Cocoa Butter 3.3 oz.
- Coconut Oil 8.3 oz.
- Olive Oil 19.8 oz.
- Sodium Hydroxide Lye- 4.6 oz.
- Distilled Water- 10.9 oz.
- Balsam Peru Essential Oil- 2 oz.
- 1 Tbsp. Beet Root Powder
- Rosehip Powder- 2 tsp.
- Blackberry Seeds

Instructions:

1. Start by slowly mixing the 4.6 ounces of lye with 10.9 ounces of distilled water. Allow them to cool down to below 100°F.
2. Take out a pan and melt your Babassu Oil, Cocoa Butter, Coconut Oil, Olive Oil. Don't overheat the oils. Whisk until they are mixed well.
3. Use a thermometer to check the temperature of the oil mixture. Ensure that it is 100°F above the lye solution.
4. While you wait for it to get to the right temperature, mix your Beet Root Powder and Rosehip Powder in a bowl. Whisk well.

5. Once the temperatures are right, mix the lye-water into the oil mixture before you add your whisked Rosehip mixture.
6. Hand-mix it before you use a stick blender to mix it well.
7. After that, add your Balsam Peru Essential Oil.
8. Put the mixture in the pre-lined mold then spray with 99% isopropyl alcohol to prevent soda ash.
9. Press your blackberry seeds on the soap bars.
10. Refrigerate them for about two days.
11. Immediately after your soap has hardened, remove it from your mold, then cut it.
12. Allow it to cure for at least 4 weeks.

Lime LaCroix Cold Process Soap

Ingredients:

- Swirl Quick Mix- 33 oz.
- Sodium Hydroxide Lye- 4.6 oz.
- Flat Lime LaCroix- 10.9 oz.
- Lime Fragrance Oil- 2.4 oz.
- Blue Slushy Mica
- Kermit Green Mica
- Hydrated Chrome Green Colorant
- Aqua Pearl Mica

- Titanium Dioxide

Instructions:

1. Start by slowly mixing the 4.6 ounces of lye with 10.9 ounces of LaCroix. Allow them to cool down to below 100°F.
2. Take out a pan and melt your Swirl Quick Mix. Don't overheat the oils. Whisk until they are mixed well.
3. Use a thermometer to check the temperature of the oil mixture. Ensure that it is 100°F above the lye solution.
4. While you wait for it to get to the right temperature, mix your Blue Slushy Mica, Kermit Green Mica, Hydrated Chrome Green Colorant, Aqua Pearl Mica and Titanium Dioxide in a bowl. Whisk well.
5. Once the temperatures are right, mix the lye-water with the oil mixture before you add your whisked Titanium Dioxide mixture.
6. Hand-mix it before you use a stick blender to mix it well.
7. After that, add your Lime Fragrance Oil.
8. Put the mixture in the pre-lined mold then spray with 99% isopropyl alcohol to prevent soda ash.
9. Press your blackberry seeds on the soap bars.
10. Refrigerate them for about two days.
11. Immediately after your soap has hardened, remove it from your mold, then cut it.

12. Allow it to cure for at least 4 weeks.

Kelly Green Cold Process Soap

Ingredients:

- Basic Quick Mix- 33 oz.
- Distilled Water- 10.9 oz.
- Sodium Hydroxide Lye- 4.7 oz.
- Sodium Lactate- 2 tsp.
- Apple Sage Fragrance Oil- 2.4 oz.
- Kelly Green Mica- 1 tsp.

Instructions:

1. Start by slowly mixing the 4.7 ounces of lye with 10.9 ounces of water. Allow them to cool down to below 100°F.
2. Take out a pan and melt your Basic Quick Mix. Don't overheat the oils. Whisk until they are mixed well.
3. Use a thermometer to check the temperature of the oil mixture. Ensure that it is 100°F above the lye solution.
4. While you wait for it to get to the right temperature, mix your Kelly Green Mica in a bowl. Whisk well.
5. Once the temperatures are right, mix the lye-water into the oil mixture before you add your whisked Kelly Green Mica- mixture.

6. Hand-mix it before you use a stick blender to mix it well.
7. After that, add your Apple Sage Fragrance Oil.
8. Put the mixture in the pre-lined mold then spray with 99% isopropyl alcohol to prevent soda ash.
9. Refrigerate them for about two days.
10. Immediately after your soap has hardened, remove it from your mold, then cut it.
11. Allow it to cure for at least 4 weeks.

Blue Handmade Cold Process Soap

Ingredients:

- Swirl Quick Mix- 33 oz.
- Distilled Water- 10.9 oz.
- Sodium Hydroxide Lye- 4.6 oz.
- Sodium Lactate- 2 tsp.
- fragrance oil- 2.4 oz.
- black colorant- ¼ tsp.
- blue colorant- ½ tsp.

Instructions:

1. Start by slowly mixing the 4.6 ounces of lye with 10.9 ounces of water. Allow them to cool down to below 100°F. Add your sodium lactate.

2. Take out a pan and melt your Swirl Quick Mix. Don't overheat the oils. Whisk until they are mixed well.

3. Use a thermometer to check the temperature of the oil mixture. Ensure that it is 100°F above the lye solution.

4. While you wait for it to get to the right temperature, mix your black colorant and blue colorant in a bowl. Whisk well.

5. Once the temperatures are right, mix the lye-water with the oil mixture before you add your whisked black colorant mixture.

6. Hand-mix it before you use a stick blender to mix it well.

7. After that, add your Fragrance Oil.

8. Put the mixture in the pre-lined mold then spray with 99% isopropyl alcohol to prevent soda ash.

9. Refrigerate them for about two days.

10. Immediately after your soap has hardened, remove it from your mold, then cut it.

11. Allow it to cure for at least 4 weeks.

Moonstone Cold Process Soap

Ingredients:

- Basic Quick Mix- 54 oz.
- Sodium Hydroxide Lye- 7.7 oz.

- Distilled Water- 15.1 oz.
- Moonstone Fragrance Oil- 3.5 oz.
- Titanium Dioxide
- Snowflake Sparkle Mica
- Aqua Pearl Mica
- Magenta Mica
- Lavender Mica
- Party Pink Mica

Instructions:

1. Start by slowly mixing the 7.7 ounces of lye with 15.1 ounces of water. Allow them to cool down to below 100°F. Add your sodium lactate.
2. Take out a pan and melt your Basic Quick Mix. Don't overheat the oils. Whisk until they are mixed well.
3. Use a thermometer to check the temperature of the oil mixture. Ensure that it is 100°F above the lye solution.
4. While you wait for it to get to the right temperature, mix your Titanium Dioxide, Snowflake Sparkle Mica, Aqua Pearl Mica, Magenta Mica, Lavender Mica and Party Pink Mica in a bowl. Whisk well.
5. Once the temperatures are right, mix the lye-water into the oil mixture before you add your whisked Titanium Dioxide mixture.
6. Hand-mix it before you use a stick blender to mix it well.

7. After that, add your Moonstone Fragrance Oil.
8. Put the mixture in the pre-lined mold then spray with 99% isopropyl alcohol to prevent soda ash.
9. Refrigerate them for about two days.
10. Immediately after your soap has hardened, remove it from your mold, then cut it.
11. Allow it to cure for at least 4 weeks.

Kokum Butter Cold Process Soap

Ingredients:

- Castor Oil 0.7 oz.
- Coconut Oil 8.5 oz.
- Kokum Butter 1.7 oz.
- Olive Oil- 23.1 oz
- Sodium Hydroxide Lye- 4.7 oz.
- Distilled Water- 10.3 oz.
- Eucalyptus Essential Oil- 2 oz.
- Titanium Dioxide
- Ground Pumpkin Seeds- 3 Tbsp.

Instructions:

1. Start by slowly mixing the 4.7 ounces of lye with 10.3 ounces of water. Allow them to cool down to below 100°F. Add your sodium lactate.

2. Take out a pan and melt your Castor Oil, Coconut Oil, Kokum Butter, and Olive Oil. Don't overheat the oils. Whisk until they are mixed well.

3. Use a thermometer to check the temperature of the oil mixture. Ensure that it is 100°F above the lye solution.

4. While you wait for it to get to the right temperature, mix your Titanium Dioxide in a bowl. Whisk well.

5. Once the temperatures are right, mix the lye-water into the oil mixture before you add your whisked Titanium Dioxide mixture.

6. Hand-mix it before you use a stick blender to mix it well.

7. After that, add your Eucalyptus Essential Oil.

8. Put the mixture in the pre-lined mold then spray with 99% isopropyl alcohol to prevent soda ash.

9. Press your ground pumpkin seeds on the soap bars.

10. Refrigerate them for about two days.

11. Immediately after your soap has hardened, remove it from your mold, then cut it.

12. Allow it to cure for at least 4 weeks.

Coffee Cold Process Soap

Ingredients:

- Swirl Recipe Quick Mix- 54 oz.
- Sodium Hydroxide Lye- 7. 5 oz.
- Plain Coffee- 17.8 oz.
- Espresso Fragrance Oil- 3 oz.
- Titanium Dioxide Pigment
- Brown Oxide Pigment
- Black Oxide Pigment
- Used Coffee Grounds- 2 Tbsp.
- Whole Espresso Beans (for the top)

Instructions:

1. Start by slowly mixing the 7.5 ounces of lye with 17.8 ounces of water. Allow them to cool down to below 100°F. Add your sodium lactate.
2. Take out a pan and melt your Swirl Recipe Quick Mix. Don't overheat the oils. Whisk until they are mixed well.
3. Use a thermometer to check the temperature of the oil mixture. Ensure that it is 100°F above the lye solution.
4. While you wait for it to get to the right temperature, mix your Titanium Dioxide Pigment, Brown Oxide Pigment, Black Oxide Pigment and Used Coffee Grounds in a bowl. Whisk well.

5. Once the temperatures are right, mix the lye-water into the oil mixture before you add your whisked Titanium Dioxide mixture.

6. Hand-mix it before you use a stick blender to mix it well.

7. After that, add your Espresso Fragrance Oil.

8. Put the mixture in the pre-lined mold then spray with 99% isopropyl alcohol to prevent soda ash.

9. Press your whole espresso beans on the soap bars.

10. Refrigerate them for about two days.

11. Immediately after your soap has hardened, remove it from your mold, then cut it.

12. Allow it to cure for at least 4 weeks.

Lavender Kombucha Cold Process Soap

Ingredients:

- Swirl Recipe Quick Mix- 39 oz.
- Sodium Hydroxide Lye 5.5 oz.
- Prepped Kombucha 11.6 oz.
- Lavender Mica
- Titanium Dioxide
- Lavender 40/42 Essential Oil- 2 oz.
- Lavender Buds

Instructions:

1. Start by slowly mixing the 5.5 ounces of lye with 11.6 ounces of Prepped Kombucha. Allow them to cool down to below 100°F. Add your sodium lactate.

2. Take out a pan and melt your Swirl Recipe Quick Mix. Don't overheat the oils. Whisk until they are mixed well.

3. Use a thermometer to check the temperature of the oil mixture. Ensure that it is 100°F above the lye solution.

4. While you wait for it to get to the right temperature, mix your Lavender Mica and

5. Titanium Dioxide in a bowl. Whisk well.

6. Once the temperatures are right, mix the lye-water into the oil mixture before you add your whisked Titanium Dioxide mixture.

7. Hand-mix it before you use a stick blender to mix it well.

8. After that, add your Lavender 40/42 Essential Oil.

9. Put the mixture in the pre-lined mold then spray with 99% isopropyl alcohol to prevent soda ash.

10. Press your Lavender buds on the soap bars.

11. Refrigerate them for about two days.

12. Immediately after your soap has hardened, remove it from your mold, then cut it.

13. Allow it to cure for at least 4 weeks.

Zesty Green Cold Process Soap

Ingredients:

- Swirl Quick Mix- 33 oz.
- Sodium Hydroxide Lye- 4.6 oz.
- Distilled Water- 10.9 oz.
- Ginger Lime Fragrance Oil- 1 oz.
- Green Salsa Fragrance Oil- 1 oz.
- Green Chrome Oxide Pigment
- Titanium Dioxide
- Green Forest Jojoba Beads- 1 Tbs.

Instructions:

1. Start by slowly mixing the 4.6 ounces of lye with 10.9 ounces of water. Allow them to cool down to below 100°F. Add your sodium lactate.
2. Take out a pan and melt your Swirl Quick Mix. Don't overheat the oils. Whisk until they are mixed well.
3. Use a thermometer to check the temperature of the oil mixture. Ensure that it is 100°F above the lye solution.
4. While you wait for it to get to the right temperature, mix your Green Chrome Oxide Pigment and Titanium Dioxide in a bowl. Whisk well.
5. Once the temperatures are right, mix the lye-water into the oil mixture before you add your whisked titanium dioxide mixture.

6. Hand-mix it before you use a stick blender to mix it well.

7. After that, add your Ginger Lime Fragrance Oil and Green Salsa Fragrance Oil.

8. Put the mixture in the pre-lined mold then spray with 99% isopropyl alcohol to prevent soda ash.

9. Press your Green Forest Jojoba Beads on the soap bars.

10. Refrigerate them for about two days.

11. Immediately after your soap has hardened, remove it from your mold, then cut it.

12. Allow it to cure for at least 4 weeks.

Energizing Orange Cold Process Soap

Ingredients:

- Lots of Lather Quick Mix- 33 oz.
- Distilled Water- 10 oz.
- Sodium Hydroxide Lye- 4.7 oz.
- Sodium Lactate- 2 tsp.
- 10X Orange Essential Oil- 1.7 oz.
- Orange Peel Powder- 3 tsp.
- Marigold Petals
- 99% Isopropyl Alcohol in Spray Bottle

Instructions:

1. Start by slowly mixing the 4.7 ounces of lye with 10 ounces of water. Allow them to cool down to below 100°F. Add your sodium lactate.
2. Take out a pan and melt your Lots of Lather Quick Mix. Don't overheat the oils. Whisk until they are mixed well.
3. Use a thermometer to check the temperature of the oil mixture. Ensure that it is 100°F above the lye solution.
4. While you wait for it to get to the right temperature, mix your Orange Peel Powder in a bowl. Whisk well.
5. Once the temperatures are right, mix the lye-water into the oil mixture before you add your whisked Orange Peel Powder mixture.
6. Hand-mix it before you use a stick blender to mix it well.
7. After that, add your 10X Orange Essential Oil.
8. Put the mixture in the pre-lined mold then spray with 99% isopropyl alcohol to prevent soda ash.
9. Press your marigold petals on the soap.
10. Refrigerate them for about two days.
11. Immediately after your soap has hardened, remove it from your mold, then cut it.
12. Allow it to cure for at least 4 weeks.

Orange & Clove Spice Cold Process Soap

Yields: 1 loaf of 3 lbs.

Ingredients

- 45 oz. Olive oil
- 32 oz. Coconut oil
- 8 oz. Castor oil
- 12 oz. Lye
- 32 oz. Distilled water
- 2 oz. Orange fold 5 essential oil
- 8 oz. Clove essential oil
- ~2-3 tsp black walnut powder

Prepare this soap batter with the normal cold process method as described. Black walnut powder is optional but gives your bar of soap a rustic decoration that compliments the musk fragrance and imitates the appearance of ground clove. Add fragrances and embellishments at the end of the process; pour into your mold and set aside. Cut in 24 – 48 hours. Allow this bar 6 weeks to cure. Remember, soap with a high content of olive oil need a little longer time to cure in order to get a better lather.

Honey & Beeswax Soap

Yields: 1 loaf of 2 lbs.

Ingredients

- 8 oz. Of water
- 4 oz. Of lye
- 10 oz. Of coconut oil
- 2 oz. Of shea butter
- 12 oz. Of olive oil
- 2 oz. Of sweet almond oil
- 2 oz. Of sunflower oil
- 1.5 oz. Honey almond fragrance oil
- 1 tbsp. Of beeswax pastilles
- 1 tbsp. Of local honey

Instructions:

Prepare this recipe with the normal cold process method described. Melt the beeswax pastilles completely in the microwave before mixing. If they are not completely liquid, they will not melt into the batter properly. Add the fragrance and honey at the very end. Honey will accelerate the trace. This will give less time to work with the soap before it hardens.

Woodland Pine Soap

Yields: 1 loaf of 2 lbs.

Ingredients

- 0 oz. Of water
- 4.1 oz. Of lye
- 12 oz. Of coconut oil
- 2 oz. Of shea butter
- 10 oz. Of olive oil
- 2 oz. Of hemp oil
- 2 oz. Of soybean oil
- 1.5 oz. Of pine fragrance oil
- 1/8 tsp of green mica
- ¼ tsp of woodland green mica
- 1 tsp of white pearl mica

Instructions:

This soap is very aesthetic with its popping colors. First start this recipe by mixing your bright colors. Take three oz. Of olive oil and separate an ounce into three cups. Mix your micas until a smooth colorant is achieved and set aside. Prepare your soap batter with the basic cold process method.

Remember, you will be mixing 7 oz. Of olive oil as you have just removed 3 oz. Once your batter is mixed. Add the fragrance. Separate your batter into three parts and color each part.

Pour each color into your mold with a drop swirl technique and give it a twist with your spoon. Set aside to harden for 24 hours before cutting.

Sweet Pear Soap

Yields: 1 loaf of 5 lbs.

Ingredients

- 22 oz. Of olive oil
- 4 oz. Of pureed dessert pears
- 18 oz. Of coconut oil
- 18 oz. Of water
- 8 oz. Of lye
- 8 oz. Of shea butter
- 8 oz. Of avocado oil
- 8 oz. Of rice bran oil
- 4 oz. Of sweet juicy pear fragrance oil
- ¼ tsp. Of lavender mica powder
- ¼ tsp. Of teal mica powder

Instructions:

First prepare your pureed pears. Mix them to a soft pulp in a texture like baby food and set aside. In the basic cold process method prepare your lye solution and oils. Mix the two parts when the temperatures both have cooled to about 100 degrees.

Mix with your stick blender until a light trace has been reached. Add your pear puree and fragrance and mix thoroughly. Split the batter into two parts and color each part. Mix into your molds with a layered and swirl technique. Give this bar large fat swirls. The fruity smell is a popular fragrance, and the fruit puree creates a smooth texture. Unmold and cut after 24 hours.

Lemongrass Swirl

Yields: 1 loaf of 4 lbs.
Ingredients

- 8 oz. Of water
- 12 oz. Of coconut oil
- 2 oz. Of shea butter
- 2 oz. Of cocoa butter
- 10 oz. Of olive oil
- 2 oz. Of hemp seed oil
- 4.1 oz. Of lye
- 1.5 oz. Of lemongrass oil / fragrance oil
- 1/4 tsp of blue mica
- 4 tsp of yellow mica

Instructions:

Make the batter with the basic cold process technique. This is a small recipe and easy to complete. Mix your lye and oils completely. Add your shea butter at the end of this process. Try to keep your trace light. Add your fragrance and split the batter into two parts. Mix your two colors. One part will have 2 tsp. Of yellow mica. The other will have 2 tsp. Of yellow and ½ tsp of blue mics. Pour the yellow part into your mold and then drop the green batter from several inches above allowing the batter to drop into the yellow color. Now swirl with your spoon for those long wispy swirls. This is called the drop swirl technique. Set your mold aside and cut this loaf after 24 hours.

Mango Butter With Ylang Ylang

Yields: 1 loaf of 1 lb.

Ingredients

- 3.2 oz. Of mango butter
- 4.8 oz. Of shea butter
- 8.5 oz. Of coconut oil
- 3 oz. Of avocado oil
- 3 oz. Of castor oil
- 9.5 oz. Of olive oil
- 10.5 oz. Of distilled water
- 4.3 oz. Of lye

- 2 oz. Of ylang ylang essential oil

Instructions:

This bar requires the basic instructions from the cold process described. Here our Ingredients are focused on the mango and ylang ylang. Allow your mango butter to the last of the oils that are blended. This will allow the super fat to be the mango butter and that will be the moisture that remains untouched by the lye. Ylang ylang is an essential oil. Remember essential oils go a long way, so no more than 2 oz. After mixing your batter you can leave this bar uncolored or you can give it a touch of floral color mica. Ylang-ylangs are yellow, so that would be fitting. Set to harden for 24 hours before cutting, and cure for 4 – 6 weeks.

Raw Honey & Dandelion Soap

- Yields: 3 bars
- Ingredients
- 14 oz. Of olive oil
- 8 oz. Of coconut oil
- 3 oz. Of sunflower oil
- 2 oz. Of shea butter
- 1.5 oz. Of jojoba oil
- 1.5 oz. Of sweet almond oil

- 10 oz. Of dandelion tea
- 4 oz. Of lye
- .5 oz. Of raw honey

Instructions:

First make your tea. The dandelions in this soap aren't special. You can get them straight from the back yard. Wash them and boil them down in a pot of water. You will get a light green water just as you do when you boil spinach. Leave the leaves in the water and let it sit in your fridge overnight.

Next make your batter in the normal cold process way. You want your jojoba to be the super fat in this recipe so blend everything well and add the jojoba as the last oil. Add your honey at the end and blend well. Honey can accelerate a batch of soap to a thicker trace more quickly, so only add it when you are ready. Set this into your mold and cut in 24 hours. This recipe will give you a lite honey grass small. Feel free to add additional flower fragrances to tweak it if necessary.

Summertime Watermelon Soap

Yields: 1 loaf of 3 lbs.

Ingredients

- Water 10.24 oz.
- Lye 6.95 oz.
- Canola 9.6 oz.
- Olive 9.6 oz.
- Coconut 16.8 oz.
- Lard 9.6 oz.
- Shea butter 2.4 oz.
- Colorant green, pink, titanium dioxide
- Fragrance watermelon 2.5 oz.
- Black large sprinkles ½ cup

Instructions:

Mix your batter in the standard cold process way. Once your oils and lye are mixed add your fragrance. You will split this batter into three bowls. Most of your batter will be colored pink. Two small bowls will be mixed with green and white separately. The green will be the first layer poured. The white will be the second layer poured. Mix your large black sprinkles into your pink batter before you pour it. Layer the pink on the top. Pour gently so that you do not disrupt the two bottom layers. One way to do this is to pour directly onto spoon to absorb the impact.

This way your batter will fall more gently. Set aside and let set for 24 hours before you cut.

Vanilla Cupcakes

Yields: 11 cupcakes
Ingredients

- water 14 oz.
- lye 7.3 oz.
- coconut oil 18.5 oz.
- lard 15 oz.
- vegetable oil 11.5 oz.
- olive oil 15 oz.
- castor oil 7.3 oz.
- shea butter 2.5 oz.
- titanium dioxide (white colorant), dark purple mica
- black cherry fragrance 2.5 oz.

Instructions:

Following the cold process procedure mix your oils in one bowl and lye in another. Give both mixtures time to cool. Mix them together, add your fragrance, and split your soap batter into two parts.

Mix thoroughly, but not too much you need to have time to work with the batter so leave it at a light trace. With the first part of the batter, mix your titanium dioxide into your bowl until you get as close to white or vanilla cake color as you like and pour into your cupcake holders. Color one bowl of batter dark purple.

Next, split the second bowl of batter into two parts again.

In the second bowl add your titanium dioxide until your batter is a lighter shade of purple.

Bring your batter to a thicker trace by mixing the batter until you can get peaks to form in the batter. Now fill your two shades of purple batter into your two frosting bags. P ipe a dark layer in a circle on each cupcake. Follow that with a smaller lighter purple layer on the top of the white, and finish with a dollop of the first frosting on the top. Let theses harden for 24 hours before you move them around.

Sage & Citrus Cold Process

Yields: 1 loaf of 3 lbs. (11 bars)

Ingredients

- 18.24 oz. Of water
- 7 oz. Of lye
- 9.6 oz. Of canola oil
- 9.6 oz. Of olive oil
- 16.8 oz. Of coconut oil
- 9.6 oz. Of lard
- 2.4 oz. Of shea butter
- ¼ tsp. Of yellow mica
- ½ tsp. Of green mica
- fragrance sage & citrus 2.5 oz.
- rosemary 3 teaspoons

Instructions:

Melt your oils together in the microwave in short bursts. Add your oil to your lye solution leaving out the shea butter. Mix your shea butter after all your other oils are thoroughly mixed together with the lye. This will allow your shea butter to be the super fat. Add your fragrances. Split the batter into two parts. Color one half ivory yellow, and the other half pastel green. Add your rosemary to the yellow half of the batter. Now you can layer the yellows and green in alternate layers. Swirl the two colors with a chopstick or spoon. Unmold after 24 hours.

Bastille Cold Process Soap

Yields: 1 loaf of 3 lbs.

Ingredients

- 12.16 oz. Water
- 4.4 oz. Lye (naoh)
- 25 oz. Olive oil
- 5 oz. Coconut oil (181.5 grams)
- 2 oz. Castor oil (45.4 grams)
- colorants can be liquid or micas
- oz. Fragrance oils of your choice

Instructions:

Clean & sanitize your work area and all of your packaging materials. Don't skip out on wearing gloves, protective clothing, a face mask, safety glasses.

Tie long hair back. Olive oil can be a heavy green color and tends to give your natural soap batter a dark yellow look. This will influence the color of your bars after you add colorant. Experiment with extra virgin olive oil or lighter olive oils for the end result colors you like the best. All olive oil makes great soap. You can work with any olive oils that you like the best.

Quick And Easy Castile Soap

Yields: 1 loaf of 2 lbs.

Ingredients

- 32 oz. Pure olive oil
- 4.12 oz. Lye (sodium hydroxide)
- 12.16 oz. Distilled water
- 1 oz. Of your favorite fragrance or essential oil
- Silicone soap (bread) mold

Instructions:

Create this recipe with the standard cold process method. Very famous as a traditional creation in castile, Spain, this recipe produces a soap with well-known characteristics. First, the final result is a very gentle product.

Castile soap is good for most skin types and especially sensitive skin and children. Additionally, it takes a long time for this soap to cure. We recommend you cure this recipe for the standard 4 – 6 weeks, but it is not uncommon for a pure castile to take 3 months and some traditional factories will let it cure for up to a year. Once cures and properly stored, this soap will last for several years on the shelves.

Turmeric Ombre

Ingredients

- 1 ½ ounces castor oil
- 2 ¼ ounces cocoa butter
- 16 ounces of coconut oil
- 7 ounces of olive oil
- 14 ounces of Babassu Oil
- 11 ounces sunflower oil
- 2 ¾ turmeric powder
- 7 ¾ ounces lye
- 16 ounces water (distilled)
- Turmeric Powder

The base

1. Use a lye calculator to determine the water and lye weights you should include. Measure the weights and mix the lye and water to form the lye solution. Remember to add lye to the water and not the reverse. Let it cool to about 90 to 110°F.
2. Combine all the oils together, heat the butter and fat and add to the oils to raise their temperature to match that of the lye.
3. Mix the oil and the lye solution. Blend until trace.

Additives

1. Once you have reached trace before pouring into the mold, add your blend of essential oils.
2. Add the turmeric powder and keep blending until well mixed.

Curing and finishing

1. Pour the batter into the prepared mold. Slightly tap the mold or use a spatula to remove any trapped air bubbles. Work quickly to avoid the batter thickening further before pouring.
2. Cover the mold and do not disturb for at least 24 hours. You can leave it for up to 48 hours the preference is yours. after 24 – 48 hours take the soap from the mold carefully. The soap is solid but not so hard.
3. Cut into small soap bars using a hand wire. You can craft into any desired shapes and add branding at this stage.
4. Let the soap sit for 4-6 weeks to harden.

Avocado Soap

Ingredients

- 33% avocado oil
- 30% Babassu Oil

- 30% palm kernel oil
- 7% sweet almond oil
- Lye
- Distilled Water
- Avocado Puree
- Rosemary extract

The base

1. Use a lye calculator to determine the water and lye weights you should include. Measure the weights and mix the lye and water to form the lye solution. Remember to add lye to the water and not the reverse. Let it cool to about 90 to 110°F.
2. Combine all the oils together, heat the oils to raise their temperature to match that of the lye.
3. Mix the oil and the lye solution. Blend until trace.

Additives

1. Once you have reached trace before pouring into the mold, add rosemary extract.
2. Add the avocado puree and keep blending until well mixed.

Curing and finishing

1. Pour the batter into the prepared mold. Slightly tap the mold or use a spatula to remove any trapped air

bubbles. Work quickly to avoid the batter thickening further before pouring.

2. Cover the mold and do not disturb for at least 24 hours. You can leave it for up to 48 hours the preference is yours. after 24 – 48 hours take the soap from the mold carefully. The soap is solid but not so hard.

3. cut into small soap bars using a hand wire. You can craft into any desired shapes and add branding at this stage.

4. Let the soap sit for 4-6 weeks to harden.

Note: the color of the soap may vary.

Tree Tea Soap

Ingredients

- 45% olive oil
- 30% coconut oil
- 13% sweet almond oil
- 12% avocado oil
- water
- sodium hydroxide lye
- tea tree essential oil

The base

1. Use a lye calculator to determine the water and lye weights you should include. Measure the weights and mix the lye and water to form the lye solution. Remember to add lye to the water and not the reverse. Let it cool to about 90 to 110°F
2. Combine all the oils together, heat the oils to raise their temperature to match that of the lye.
3. Mix the oil and the lye solution. Blend until trace.

Additives

- Add the tea tree essential oil and keep blending until well mixed.

Curing and finishing

1. Pour the batter into the prepared mold. Slightly tap the mold or use a spatula to remove any trapped air bubbles. Work quickly to avoid the batter thickening further before pouring.
2. Cover the mold and do not disturb for at least 24 hours. You can leave it for up to 48 hours the preference is yours. after 24 – 48 hours take the soap from the mold carefully. The soap is solid but not so hard.
3. cut into small soap bars using a hand wire. You can craft into any desired shapes and add branding at this stage.
4. Let the soap sit for 4-6 weeks to harden.

Shea Butter Soap

Ingredients

- 50% olive oil
- 20% coconut oil
- 25% Babassu Oil
- 5% shea butter
- water
- sodium hydroxide lye
- tea tree essential oil

The base

1. Use a lye calculator to determine the water and lye weights you should include. Measure the weights and mix the lye and water to form the lye solution. Remember to add lye to the water and not the reverse. Let it cool to about 90°F to 110°F.
2. Combine all the oils together, heat the oils to raise their temperature to match that of the lye.
3. Mix the oil and the lye solution. Blend until trace.

Additives

1. Add the tea tree essential oil and keep blending until well mixed.

Curing and finishing

1. Pour the batter into the prepared mold. Slightly tap the mold or use a spatula to remove any trapped air bubbles. Work quickly to avoid the batter thickening further before pouring.

2. Cover the mold and do not disturb for at least 24 hours You can leave it for up to 48 hours the preference is yours. after 24 – 48 hours take the soap from the mold carefully. The soap is solid but not so hard.

3. Cut into small soap bars using a hand wire. You can craft into any desired shapes and add branding at this stage.

4. Let the soap sit for 4-6 weeks to harden.

Hibiscus Infused Soap

Yields: 1 loaf of 2 lbs.

Ingredients

- 4.3 oz. Of lye
- 8.6 oz. Of water
- 12 oz. Of coconut oil
- 4 oz. Of shea butter
- 10 oz. Of olive oil
- 4 oz. Of rice bran oil
- 2 oz. Of red hibiscus & acai fragrance oil
- 1/2cup of hibiscus flowers

- 1 ¼ tsp. Of crimson sparkle mica

Instructions:

The first step in this soap recipe is to make an infused tea with your water and ¼ cups of your flower petals. Simmer your petals in two cups of water. You can expect that you will lose water through evaporation. The end result should leave you with your desired 8.6 oz. Of water. After your petals are boiled down, put the water in the fridge with the petals until the water is cold. When you are ready to make your lye solution, strain the petals out of the water before mixing the lye crystals. Set your solution aside to cool. Mix your oils. Blend you oils and lye with the basic cold process method and add your fragrance, colorant, and remaining petals. Pour into your mold and allow to harden for 24 hours.

Lemon Peel & Blueberry Yogurt Soap

Yields: 1 loaf of 2 lbs.

Ingredients

- 12 oz. Of coconut oil
- 10 oz. Of apricot kernel oil
- 6 oz. Of olive oil
- 7 oz. Of shea butter
- 2 oz. Of castor oil

- 5 oz. Of lye
- 6.3 oz. Of water
- 4 oz. Of yogurt
- 22 grams lemon essential oil
- 1 oz. Of blueberry fragrance oil
- 1 teaspoon alkanet root
- 1 teaspoon lemon zest or lemon peel powder
- 1/2 teaspoon blueberry seeds

Instructions:

Prepare your alkanet root by softening the powder. This will give you a natural purple dye. Mix one ounce of any soft oil with your alkanet root and set it aside. Prepare your soap batter by mixing your lye solution and oils with the cold process method that you have learned. Add your yogurt after your oils and lye are mixed well. Split your batter in half. Mix your natural colorant in one half of the batter and mix this with your blueberry fragrance oil. In the other bowl add your blueberry seeds, lemon zest, and lemon essential oil. Layer the two parts of soap batter in your mold in alternating layers. Use a spoon to swirl the batter into a beautiful pattern. Set this aside to harden for 24 hours. Cut and allow this soap to cure for 3 – 6 weeks.

Chapter 12: Hot Process Soap Recipes

Coconut Soap

Ingredients

- 25% Babassu Oil
- 25% Sweet Almond Oil
- 20% Coconut Oil
- 20% Olive Oil
- 5% Castor Oil
- 5% Cocoa Butter
- Lye
- water
- Coconut Milk

The base

1. Use a lye calculator to determine the water and lye weights you should include. Measure the weights and mix the lye and water to form the lye solution. Remember to add lye to the water and not the reverse. Let it cool to about 90 to 110°F

2. Combine all the oils together in a crockpot. heat the oils to raise their temperature to match that of the lye.

3. Mix the oil and the lye solution. Blend until trace.

4. Cover the crockpot and cook in low heat. After 10-15 minutes observe if there is any color change. If the middle is still white stir and let it sit for some more minutes. The amount of batter increases in size as it cooks. Cooking time is dependent on the size and shape of the crockpot

Additives

1. Once the batter turns gel-like add the essential oils and stir with a wooden spatula.

2. Add the coconut milk and keep blending until well mixed.

Curing and finishing

1. Pour the batter into the prepared mold. Slightly tap the mold or use a spatula to remove any trapped air bubbles. Work quickly to avoid the batter thickening further before pouring.

2. Cover the mold and do not disturb for at least 24 hours. You can leave it for up to 48 hours the preference is yours. after 24 – 48 hours take the soap from the mold carefully. The soap is solid but not so hard.

3. cut into small soap bars using a hand wire. You can craft into any desired shapes and add branding at this stage.
4. The soap is ready for use as soon as it is cut. However, leaving it to cool for some time can make it even better.

Aloe Vera Soap

Ingredients

- 20% Coconut Oil
- 20% Olive Oil
- 5% Castor Oil
- 5% Shea Butter
- Lye
- water
- aloe gel

The base

1. Use a lye calculator to determine the water and lye weights you should include. Measure the weights and mix the lye and water to form the lye solution. Remember to add lye to the water and not the reverse. Let it cool to about 90 to 110°F
2. Combine all the oils together in a crockpot. heat the oils to raise their temperature to match that of the lye.

3. Mix the oil and the lye solution. Blend until trace.

4. Cover the crockpot and cook in low heat. After 10-15 minutes observe if there is any color change. If the middle is still white stir and let it sit for some more minutes. The amount of batter increases in size as it cooks. Cooking time is dependent on the size and shape of the crockpot

Additives

1. Once the batter turns gel-like add the essential oils and stir with a wooden spatula.

2. Add the avocado puree and keep blending until well mixed.

Curing and finishing

1. Pour the batter into the prepared mold. Slightly tap the mold or use a spatula to remove any trapped air bubbles. Work quickly to avoid the batter thickening further before pouring.

2. Cover the mold and do not disturb for at least 24 hours. You can leave it for up to 48 hours the preference is yours. after 24 – 48 hours take the soap from the mold carefully. The soap is solid but not so hard.

3. cut into small soap bars using a hand wire. You can craft into any desired shapes and add branding at this stage.

4. The soap is ready for use as soon as it is cut. However, leaving it to cool for some time can make it even better.

African Black Soap

Ingredients

- 55% unrefined shea butter
- 30% Babassu Oil
- 15% coconut oil
- Water
- Lye
- 2 teaspoons of African black soap mixture

The base

1. Use a lye calculator to determine the water and lye weights you should include. Measure the weights and mix the lye and water to form the lye solution. Remember to add lye to the water and not the reverse. Let it cool to about 90 to 110°F
2. Combine all the oils together in a crockpot. heat the oils to raise their temperature to match that of the lye.
3. Mix the oil and the lye solution. Blend until trace.
4. Cover the crockpot and cook in low heat. After 10-15 minutes observe if there is any color change. If the middle is still white stir and let it sit for some more

minutes. The amount of batter increases in size as it cooks. Cooking time is dependent on the size and shape of the crockpot.

Additives

- Once the batter turns gel-like add the African black soap mixture and stir with a wooden spatula.

Curing and finishing

1. Pour the batter into the prepared mold. Slightly tap the mold or use a spatula to remove any trapped air bubbles. Work quickly to avoid the batter thickening further before pouring.
2. Cover the mold and do not disturb for at least 24 hours. You can leave it for up to 48 hours the preference is yours. after 24 – 48 hours take the soap from the mold carefully. The soap is solid but not so hard.
3. cut into small soap bars using a hand wire. You can craft into any desired shapes and add branding at this stage.
4. The soap is ready for use as soon as it is cut. However, leaving it to cool for some time can make it even better.

Cucumber Soap

Ingredients

- 15 ounces of sunflower oil
- 30 ounces of coconut oil
- 27 ounces of olive oil
- 21 ounces of Babassu Oil
- 5 ounces of shea butter
- 18 ounces of cucumber juice
- 540g of water
- 400g of lye (NaOH)

The base

1. Use a lye calculator to determine the water and lye weights you should include. Measure the weights and mix the lye and water to form the lye solution. Remember to add lye to the water and not the reverse. Let it cool to about 90 to 110°F
2. Combine all the oils together in a crockpot. heat the oils to raise their temperature to match that of the lye.
3. Mix the oil and the lye solution. Blend until trace.
4. Cover the crockpot and cook in low heat. After 10-15 minutes observe if there is any color change. If the middle is still white stir and let it sit for some more minutes. The amount of batter increases in size as it

cooks. Cooking time is dependent on the size and shape of the crockpot

Additives

- Once the batter turns gel-like add the cucumber oil and stir with a wooden spatula.

Curing and finishing

1. Pour the batter into the prepared mold. Slightly tap the mold or use a spatula to remove any trapped air bubbles. Work quickly to avoid the batter thickening further before pouring.
2. Cover the mold and do not disturb for at least 24 hours. You can leave it for up to 48 hours the preference is yours. after 24 – 48 hours take the soap from the mold carefully. The soap is solid but not so hard.
3. cut into small soap bars using a hand wire. You can craft into any desired shapes and add branding at this stage.
4. The soap is ready for use as soon as it is cut. However, leaving it to cool for some time can make it even better.

Herbal Soap

Ingredients

- 25% coconut oil
- 20% jojoba oil
- 28% sunflower oil infused with lavender
- 10% Babassu Oil
- 2% stearic acid
- 15% avocado oil
- lye
- distilled water
- 3% of the total batch weight essential oil blend of fennel, spearmint, marjoram, and lavender essential oils.

The base

1. Use a lye calculator to determine the water and lye weights you should include. Measure the weights and mix the lye and water to form the lye solution. Remember to add lye to the water and not the reverse. Let it cool to about 90 to 110 °F.
2. Combine all the oils together in a crockpot. heat the oils to raise their temperature to match that of the lye.
3. Mix the oil and the lye solution. Blend until trace.
4. Cover the crockpot and cook in low heat. After 10-15 minutes observe if there is any color change. If the

middle is still white stir and let it sit for some more minutes. The amount of batter increases in size as it cooks. Cooking time is dependent on the size and shape of the crockpot.

Additives

- Once the batter turns gel-like add the essential oils and stir with a wooden spatula.

Curing and finishing.

1. Pour the batter into the prepared mold. Slightly tap the mold or use a spatula to remove any trapped air bubbles. Work quickly to avoid the batter thickening further before pouring.
2. Cover the mold and do not disturb for at least 24 hours. You can leave it for up to 48 hours the preference is yours. after 24 – 48 hours take the soap from the mold carefully. The soap is solid but not so hard.
3. cut into small soap bars using a hand wire. You can craft into any desired shapes and add branding at this stage.
4. The soap is ready for use as soon as it is cut. However, leaving it to cool for some time can make it even better.

Basic Hot-Process Soap

This recipe makes a basic kitchen soap. A good kitchen soap should do a number of things. First, it should clean your hands gently. Second, it should be able to remove grease and food residue. Third, is should have some deodorizing properties. Additionally, it can be colored and scented to go with your kitchen.

Ingredients:

Yields 3 pounds

- 1 pound, 3 ounces olive oil
- 3 ounces palm kernel oil
- 10 ounces coconut oil
- 1.5 ounces castor oil
- 10 ounces water
- 4.5 ounces lye
- Your choice of scent materials
- Your choice of color
- Your choice of other additives

Instructions:

1. Combine and melt the olive oil, palm kernel oil, coconut oil, and castor oil in the slow cooker.
2. Measure the water into a heatproof mixing container. Slowly add the lye to prepare the lye solution. Pour the

hot lye solution into the oils, slowly and carefully. Stir to trace.

3. Cook in slow cooker, 3 hours on low setting. Check for consistency every 30 minutes. Check ph. Add scent materials, color, and other additives when neutral.

4. Fill molds, let cool, and set. Unmold, cut into bars, and store as usual.

Coffee Kitchen Soap

It is common soap making lore that ground coffee has a deodorizing effect on the skin. Coffee is said to be able to remove the odors of garlic and onions from your hands. You'll have to see for yourself. But there is definitely a useful scrubbing action from the ground coffee.

Ingredients:

Yields 3 pounds

- 2-pound batch recipe of your choice, substituting strong brewed coffee for the water
- 2 tablespoons finely ground coffee

Instructions:

1. Make a 2-pound batch, substituting strong brewed coffee for the water. Stir to a good medium trace.

2. Cook as usual. Check pH. If it's still caustic, continue cooking until the soap is neutral.

3. Stir the finely ground coffee into the neutral soap.

4. Pack into molds, let cool, and set. Unmold, cut into bars, and store as usual.

Lemon/Baking Soda Kitchen Soap

Lemons have long been prized for their ability to reduce kitchen odors, as has baking soda. Baking soda is also a gentle abrasive. Lemon zest helps cut grease and adds a fresh lemon scent.

Ingredients:

Yields 3 pounds

- 2-pound batch recipe of your choice
- 2 tablespoons lemon zest
- 3 tablespoons baking soda

Instructions:

1. Make up the batch as usual and stir to a good medium trace.

2. Cook as usual until the soap is neutral. Check pH. Continue cooking if it's still caustic and check again.

3. Stir the lemon zest and baking soda into the neutral soap.

4. Pack into molds, let cool, and set. Unmold, cut into bars, and store as usual.

Super-Clean Kitchen Soap

The cleaning power of this soap starts with the blend of essential oils. Orange, eucalyptus, and lavender essential oils are great grease cutters. These essential oils are also known for their reported antibacterial properties. Cornmeal adds brisk abrasive action.

Ingredients:

Yields 3 pounds

- 2-pound batch recipe of your choice
- 2 tablespoons yellow cornmeal
- 1 teaspoon orange essential oil
- 1 teaspoon eucalyptus essential oil
- 1 teaspoon lavender essential oil

Instructions:

1. Make up the batch as usual and stir to a good medium trace.
2. Cook as usual until the soap is neutral. Check pH. Continue cooking if it's still caustic and check again.

3. Stir the yellow cornmeal into the neutral soap. Add the orange essential oil, eucalyptus essential oil, and lavender essential oil. Stir well.
4. Pack into molds, let cool, and set. Unmold, cut into bars, and store as usual.

Peppermint Bath Soap

Every tub should have at least one good bath soap. Single essential oils can make for an easy choice in the morning. Choose peppermint for a brisk awakening.

Ingredients:

Yields 3 pounds

- 2-pound batch recipe of your choice, substituting strong mint tea—made from fresh peppermint, mint tea bags, or loose tea, strained well and cooled—for the water
- 1 tablespoon mint, dried and ground (you can use the contents of a mint tea bag)
- ½ teaspoon peppermint essential oil

Instructions:

1. Make up the batch as usual and stir to a good medium trace.
2. Cook as usual until the soap is neutral. Check pH. Continue cooking if it's still caustic.

3. Stir the mint into the neutral soap. Just before you pack the soap into the molds, add the peppermint essential oil. (Wait as long as possible to stir in the essential oil. It is extremely volatile—readily vaporized—and your house will smell like an explosion in a toothpaste factory.)

4. Pack into molds, let cool, and set. Unmold, cut into bars, and store as usual.

Lavender Bath Soap

To make the lavender infusion called for in this recipe, use 2 tablespoons of lavender for each cup of water in the recipe. Heat the water and pour it over the lavender. Let cool completely, then strain out the lavender. Remeasure. Add more water to compensate for any volume that may have been lost due to evaporation.

Ingredients:

Yields 3 pounds

- 2-pound batch recipe of your choice, substituting a lavender infusion for the water
- 1 tablespoon dried lavender flowers
- 1 teaspoon lavender essential oil

Instructions:

1. Make up the batch as usual and stir to a good medium trace.
2. Cook as usual until the soap is neutral. Check pH. Continue cooking if it's still caustic.
3. Stir the lavender flowers into the neutral soap. Add the lavender essential oil and stir completely.
4. Pack into molds, let cool, and set. Unmold, cut into bars, and store as usual.

Eucalyptus Bath Soap

Eucalyptus soap is a great choice for when you're feeling under the weather. To make the yarrow infusion called for in this recipe, use 2 tablespoons of yarrow for each cup of water in the recipe. Heat the water and pour it over the yarrow. Let cool completely, then strain out the yarrow. Remeasure. Add more water to compensate for any volume that may have been lost due to evaporation.

Ingredients:

Yields 3 pounds

- 2-pound batch recipe of your choice, substituting a yarrow infusion for the water
- 1 tablespoon dried yarrow (remove stems and stiff parts)
- 1 teaspoon eucalyptus essential oil

Instructions:

1. Make up the batch as usual and stir to a good medium trace.
2. Cook as usual until the soap is neutral. Check pH. Continue cooking if it's still caustic.
3. Stir the yarrow into the neutral soap. Add the eucalyptus essential oil and stir completely.
4. Pack into molds, let cool, and set. Unmold, cut into bars, and store as usual.

Rosemary Bath Soap

Rosemary is great for mental focus. To make the rosemary infusion called for in this recipe, use 2 tablespoons of rosemary for each cup of water in the recipe. Heat the water and pour it over the rosemary. Let cool, then strain out the rosemary. Remeasure. Add more water to compensate for any volume that may have been lost due to evaporation.

Ingredients:

Yields 3 pounds

- 2-pound batch recipe of your choice, substituting a rosemary infusion for the water
- 1 tablespoon finely chopped fresh rosemary leaves
- 1 teaspoon rosemary essential oil

Instructions:

1. Make up the batch as usual and stir to a good medium trace.
2. Cook as usual until the soap is neutral. Check pH. Continue cooking if it's still caustic.
3. Stir the rosemary leaves into the neutral soap. Add the rosemary essential oil and stir completely.
4. Pack into molds, let cool, and set. Unmold, cut into bars, and store as usual.

Soap for Dry Skin

Ingredients:

- 5 ounces olive oil
- 5 ounces coconut oil
- 3 ounces shea butter
- 3 ounces avocado oil
- 0.5-ounce castor oil
- 5.5 ounces water
- 1 tablespoon dried chamomile
- 2.25 ounces lye
- 10 drops German chamomile essential oil
- 5 drops rose Otto essential oil
- 2 drops jasmine essential oil

- 5 drops palmarosa essential oil

Instructions:

1. Combine and melt the olive oil, coconut oil, shea butter, castor oil, and avocado oil in the slow cooker.
2. Make a chamomile infusion by heating the water and pouring it over the dried chamomile. Let cool, then strain out the chamomile. Remeasure. Add more water to make 5.5 ounces, to compensate for any volume that may have been lost due to evaporation.
3. Place the chamomile infusion in a heatproof mixing container. Slowly add the lye to prepare the lye solution. Heat the oils and cool the lye solution to 110°F. Pour the lye solution into the oils, slowly and carefully. Stir to trace.
4. Cook in slow cooker, 3 hours on low setting. Check for consistency every 30 minutes. Check pH after 3 hours is up.
5. When the soap is neutral, add the essential oils and stir thoroughly.
6. Pack into molds, let cool, and set. Unmold, cut into bars, and store as usual.

Soap for Skin That's Not Too Oily nor Too Dry

Ingredients:

- 8 ounces olive oil
- 4 ounces coconut oil
- 4 ounces macadamia nut oil
- 0.5-ounce castor oil
- 5.5 ounces water
- 1 tablespoon dried lavender
- 2.25 ounces lye
- 5 drops German chamomile essential oil
- 2 drops rose Otto essential oil
- 1/8 teaspoon lavender essential oil

Instructions:

1. Combine and melt the olive oil, coconut oil, macadamia nut oil, and castor oil in the slow cooker.
2. Make a lavender infusion by heating the water and pouring it over the dried lavender. Let cool completely, then strain out the lavender. Remeasure. Add more water to make 5.5 ounces, to compensate for any volume that may have been lost due to evaporation.
3. Place the lavender infusion in a heatproof mixing container. Slowly add the lye to prepare the lye solution

and stir until clear. Pour the lye solution into the oils, slowly and carefully. Stir to trace.

4. Cook in slow cooker, 3 hours on low setting. Check for consistency every 30 minutes. Check pH.

5. When the soap is neutral, add the essential oils and stir thoroughly.

6. Pack into molds, let cool, and set. Unmold, cut into bars, and store as usual.

Bastille Baby Soap

Very good for those with sensitive skin.

Ingredients and equipment:

For soap:

- 2.05 ounces Shea butter
- 14.35 ounces olive oil
- 3.1 ounces coconut oil
- 1.05 ounces castor oil
- 5.3 ounces distilled water
- 2.74 ounces lye
- ¾ teaspoon salt
- 1 teaspoon sugar
- 0.6-ounce lavender essential oil

For protection:

- A pair of safety goggles
- Waterproof long sleeves clothes that are easily removable
- Long pants
- A pair of rubber gloves
- Apron

For preparing and storing:

- Weighing scale
- A large soap pots
- Thermometer
- Immersion blender
- Loaf pan soap mold
- Few small glass containers, like beakers
- A glass pitcher with a lid
- A glass pitcher without lid
- Spoon and spatula

Instructions:

1. Wear your protection gear: Wear long sleeves, long pants, apron, goggles, and gloves before starting the process of making soap. Remove it only after the process is over.
2. Make sure that the area that you are working is well aerated. Keep the windows open. Keep children away from this area during the entire process.

3. Have all the equipment close by on your countertop.

4. Make sure to weigh all the solids and liquids on the weighing scale. Also, the weighing scale should show zero before weighing each ingredient. Weigh out all the Ingredients, one at a time. Pour oils, after weighing, into different glass containers.

5. Pour water, after weighing, into the pitcher with lid.

6. Once you are done with weighing the oils and water, start off with the soap making process: Place the pitcher without a lid on the weighing scale. Weigh out the lye in the pitcher. Carefully and slowly pour the lye into the pitcher of water. Make sure that lye goes into the water and not the other way around.

7. Stir with the spoon until well combined. Keep your face away from the harmful fumes.

8. Add salt and sugar and stir until sugar dissolves. Quickly wash the spoon. Close the pitcher with the lid. Set aside in a safe place to cool.

9. Place the soap pot over a medium-low flame. Add coconut oil and Shea butter. Keep stirring gently until the oil and butter melt completely. Keep checking the temperature of the oils with the thermometer.

10. When the oil temperature reaches 110 ° F, remove the pot from heat. Add olive oil and castor oil and stir.

11. When both the oil mixture and lye are showing around 100 ° F on the thermometer, it is time to pour the lye.

12. Slowly pour the lye solution into the soap pot containing the oil mixture.

13. Using an immersion blender (do not plug it in), whisk the mixture. As soon as the oils and lye solution are mixed, the mixture begins to turn opaque. This is when saponification starts. This means the mixture will turn into soap.

14. Now plug in the immersion blender. Give short pulses of 5 – 6 seconds. Unplug and stir again with the blender.

15. Repeat the previous step a few times until the lye solution and the oils are completely mixed and emulsified. Add lavender essential oil and stir until well combined.

16. Transfer the soap into mold. Preferably line the mold with parchment paper. It is not needed for silicone molds. Run a rubber spatula on the top of the soap to make it smooth and even. Tap the molds lightly on your countertop to remove any air bubbles. Place the molds in a warm area for about 24 hours or until the soap is set.

17. Remove the soap from the mold and cut into bars. You should get about 1 ¾ pounds of soap.

18. Place the bars on a rack (like the racks you find in a store), in a well-aerated place for about 2 weeks. This is curing the soap.

19. Once cured, you are free to use the soap. You can continue keeping the cured soaps on the rack or place them in a plastic container.

Chapter 13: Melt And Pour Soap Recipes

Shea Butter And Cocoa Butter Soap

This is a very luxurious soap that will benefit your skin and your health. It is very luscious and has a great smell. It is super easy to make and will last for a long time. It is safe both for adults and for children, and with the natural Ingredients that go into the creation of this particular soap, it is unlikely to cause any allergies.

Equipment:

- Bowls
- 1 mold (large)
- Silicon spatula
- Knife
- Hand blender
- Small spoon (for decoration)

Ingredients:

- Lard – 250 gr
- Coconut oil – 140 gr
- Shea butter – 200 gr

- Olive oil – 100 gr
- Lye – 150 gr
- Water – 200 gr
- Essential oil (of your choice) – 1 teaspoon

Instructions:

1. Put the butters and the lard into a bowl and melt them in the microwave for about 30 seconds. Melt them for longer if needed to make sure that they are the right consistency.
2. Mix them together with a spoon to combine them evenly.
3. Add all of the oils into another bowl and stir them evenly.
4. Add the essential oil of your choice to the oil bowl and stir again.
5. Mix everything together in a big bowl.
6. Use a hand blender to achieve the right consistency for soap.
7. Pour the mixture into one large mold.
8. Leave the soap inside the mold for 24 hours.
9. When the soap has properly hardened, remove it from the mold.
10. Use the small spoon to create decorations across the soap. You can do this by dragging the spoon over the soap to create zig zag marks.

11. With a knife, cut the soap into thick slices.

12. Return the soap in a dark and dry place and leave it for two weeks to harden and for the water to evaporate.

Cinnamon And Cocoa Butter Soap

This is an excellent soap to make for the winter season. It has a delicious cinnamon and cocoa smell, and it is easy to make. The essence or fragrance oils that you add to this soap recipe will determine how strong the scent is, so make sure to start with a small amount (even smaller than the recipe tells you) and then add the rest if you don't think that the scent is strong enough. Some people also love to add a splash of vanilla fragrance oil for a more dessert scent; however, this is not included in this particular recipe.

Equipment:

- Bowls
- Knife
- Silicon spatula
- Long rectangular mold
- Hand blender

Ingredients:

- Castor oil – 200 gr
- Cocoa butter – 150 gr

179

- Coconut oil – 160 gr
- Olive oil – 120 gr
- Lye – 200 gr
- Water – 130 gr
- Cinnamon essence oil   1 teaspoon

Instructions:

1. Place the fragrance oil into a separate small bowl.
2. Carefully mix the lye and the water together. Gently stir with the spatula until they are mixed well together.
3. Melt the coca butter in the microwave for about 30 seconds, or however long it takes to get it to the right consistency.
4. Add the butter and all the other oils into a new bowl and mix them all together with the spatula.
5. Combine everything together into a large bowl.
6. Use a hand mixer to blend everything together until you achieve the right consistency.
7. Pour the mixture into the mold.
8. Let the soap sit in the mold for three days.
9. Remove the soap from the mold and cut it up into your desired slices.
10. Place the soap into a dark and dry place and wait for about four weeks before using the soap.

Honey and Milk Soap

This is a lovely soap that smells absolutely delicious! It is very easy to make, and it is also a recipe that will last for a very long time. The soap will also not break down too quickly, and it doesn't leave any particles behind for cleaning. It's very moisturizing for your skin and it works especially well for people who have sensitive skin.

Equipment:

- Bowls
- Silicon spatula
- Honeycomb mold
- Hand blender

Ingredients:

- Milk base soap base – 500 gr
- Honey – 5 tablespoons

Instructions:

1. Melt the soap base in the microwave for about 30 seconds or however long it takes to melt it to a liquid texture.
2. Add the honey to the mixture and stir until everything is properly combined.
3. Pour the mixture into the honeycomb molds.
4. Let the soap cool for about two hours.

5. Remove the soaps from their molds and leave them to dry for another 48 hours before using them.

Shea Butter And Lemon Soup

Some people think that this might be a strange combination because it combines shea butter with lemon. The reason why this is strange is because both of these Ingredients have a very strong scent of their own, so one will usually overpower the other. However, this is a great combination during the hot months, because your skin still needs the right hydration and yet you also want to make sure that the lemon provides you with a refreshing scent.

Equipment:

- Bowls
- Silicon spatula
- Individual soap molds
- Hand blender

Ingredients:

- Shea butter soap base – 500 gr
- Food color of your choice – 1 teaspoon
- Lemon essential oil – 2 teaspoons

Instructions:

1. Add the pre-made soap base to a microwave bowl.
2. Melt it in the microwave in 30 second increments until the mixture is completely smooth.
3. Leave the mixture to cool a little.
4. Add the food color of your choice and make sure that everything is mixed together properly.
5. Next add the essential oil and stir it all together until smooth.
6. Pour the mixture into the molds.
7. Leave the soap in the mold for 24 hours.
8. Remove the soaps from the molds and leave them in a dark and dry place.
9. Wait for about three weeks before you use them.

Oatmeal And Goat's Milk Soap

This is a very special soap when it comes to nourishing skin. Yes, it will have a beautiful and clean scent, but most importantly, this is the kind of soap that will hydrate your skin and that be used by all members of your family without any worries about allergies or skin irritations.

This is also the kind of soap that parents really love to use on their children because they made the soap on their own and they know exactly which Ingredients went into it.

There are currently so many different soaps for children on the market, but many of them have Ingredients that parents can't even pronounce, let alone want to use on their children. So, if you are looking for great organic skincare, this recipe is definitely for you!

Equipment:

- Bowls
- Silicon spatula
- Individual soap molds
- Hand blender

Ingredients:

- Honey – 2 tablespoons
- Goat's milk soap base – 500 gr
- Oats – 100 gr
- Almond essential oil – 1 teaspoon
- Vitamin E capsule – 2 capsules

Instructions:

1. Start by placing the pre-made goat's milk base soap into a bowl that you can use in the microwave.
2. Melt it in the microwave until it is completely liquid. Then let it cool a little to the side.
3. Add the raw oats into the mixture.

4. Using a spatula, gently mix in the oats into the mixture. Make sure that you have everything combined together properly.
5. Add the almond essential oil and the Vitamin E capsules.
6. Using the spatula, mix everything together until the Vitamin E capsules dissolve completely.
7. Pour the soap into the molds.
8. Let the molds sit for 48 hours.

Aloe Vera Soap

This is a great face soap recipe. Although you can certainly use this soap all over your body, aloe Vera is especially great for the skin on your face. It is famous for being able to rejuvenate your skin and to help with acne and skin redness. What's even better about this recipe is that you will be using a real aloe Vera plant to make it! Many people grow aloe Vera in their home, but if you are not one of these people, you can easily find this plant in the plant section of a larger grocery store.

Equipment:

- Bowls
- Silicon spatula
- Individual soap molds
- Hand blender

Ingredients:

- Water – 200 gr
- Aloe Vera – 50 gr
- Lye – 300 gr
- Olive oil – 150 gr
- Coconut oil – 90 gr

Instructions:

1. Combine the water and the lye into a bowl. As always, make sure that you do this very carefully and that you take care of your eyes, your lungs and your skin.
2. Mix the oils together in another bowl until everything is properly combined together.
3. Pour the oils into the lye and water mixture.
4. Using the hand blender, combine the two mixtures together until you get the consistency that you like.
5. Pour the mixture into individual soap molds and leave them for 48 hours.
6. Remove the soaps from the molds.
7. Leave them in a dark and dry place for three weeks before using.

Bubble Bath Bar

This is another very interesting soap recipe and one that is easy and fun to make. Bubble bath bars are a little different than bath bombs, because they don't have the fizzy effect. Instead, the bubble bath bar with gradually dissolve in the water, making it creamy looking and very gentle for your skin. Another great thing about the bubble bath bars is that you can easily add Ingredients that you love to them, and you can make them as healthy and as fun for your bubble bath as you want. For now, here is a very simple recipe to create your own bubble bath bars that you can get started with right away!

Equipment:

- Bowls
- Silicon spatula
- Individual soap molds
- Hand blender

Ingredients:

- Baking soda – 200 grams
- Essential oil of your choice – 1 teaspoon
- Coconut oil – 100 gr
- Liquid soap or bubble bath – 100 gr
- Corn starch – 100 gr
- Food color – a few drops

Instructions:

1. Mix all the dry Ingredients together until everything is evenly combined.
2. Add all of the liquid Ingredients into it but leave out the essential oil and the food color.
3. Stir everything until you get a creamy, even mixture.
4. Pour the mixture into the individual soap molds of your choice.
5. Leave the soap to harden for about 48 hours.
6. Remove the soup from the molds.
7. Put the molds in a dark and dry place and leave them for about two weeks before using.

Gentle Baby And Toddler Soap

Ingredients and equipment:

- 5.29 ounces Goat's milk melt and pour soap
- ½ teaspoon organic calendula extract
- ½ teaspoon hydrolyzed oats
- 20 drops tangerine essential oil

For preparing and storing:

- A pair of disposable gloves
- Apron

- Weighing scale
- Wax paper
- 2 small, silicone soap molds
- Funnel pitcher (microwave safe)
- Knife
- Spatula
- Cling wrap
- Cutting board

Instructions:

1. Wear the apron and gloves. Place all the equipment and Ingredients close to you on your countertop.
2. Weigh the Ingredients one at a time. Make sure that the weighing scale shows zero before measuring each ingredient.
3. Place the cutting board on your countertop. Place the wax paper over the cutting board. Place the soap base on the wax paper and chop into ½ inch pieces.
4. Lift the wax paper along with the soap pieces and pour into the funnel pitcher. Place the pitcher in the microwave and cook on high for 1 – 2 minutes or until it melts. Stir every 30 seconds until it almost melts after which, stir every 10 seconds until it just melts.
5. Stir in the essential oil and stir. Cook in the microwave for 10 to 20 seconds if required, stirring after 10 seconds.

6. Transfer the soap mixture into the soap molds or use one larger mold. This is done to remove extra bubbles. Set the molds aside for 12 – 24 hours.

7. Remove the soap from the molds (wearing gloves). In case the soap is not coming out of the molds easily, freeze for 60 – 70 minutes. It will come out easily.

8. Wrap each bar in cling wrap and store. The wrapping is necessary because, in humid weather, it tends to sweat.

Chapter 14: Liquid Soap Recipes

Moisturizing Antibacterial Soap

Ingredients and equipment:

- Liquid castile soap, as required
- Distilled water or boiled water, as required
- 2 tablespoons vegetable glycerin
- 4 tablespoons almond oil
- 30 drops lavender oil
- 20 drops tea tree oil
- 20 drops cedarwood oil
- 16 ounces pump bottle

Instructions:

1. First, pour enough Castile oil to fill the pump bottle up to ½ the bottle.
2. Next, pour almond oil followed by glycerin. Next, add the essential oils.
3. Now pour enough water to fill the bottle, up to 1 inch below the neck of the bottle.

4. Fasten the cap and shake the bottle until well combined.

Liquid Hand Soap with Fragrance Variations

Ingredients and equipment:

For soap:

- ½ cup liquid castile soap
- 2 cups distilled water
- 2 tablespoons fractionated coconut oil
- 24 ounces pump bottle
- Fragrance variation # 1:
- 8 drops cypress essential oil
- 10 drops sandalwood essential oil
- 10 drops white fir essential oil

Fragrance variation # 2:

- 3 tablespoons rose water
- 1 teaspoon beetroot powder (optional
- 2 tablespoons vegetable glycerin

Fragrance variation # 3:

- 12 drops lime essential oil

- 12 drops grapefruit essential oil
- 6 drops orange essential oil

Fragrance variation # 4

- 12 drops ylang-ylang essential oil
- 18 drops peppermint oil

Fragrance variation # 5:

- 30 drops any of your favorite essential oils (you can use a combination of oils)

Instructions:

1. Pour castile soap into the pump bottle. Next, add the coconut oil followed by distilled water.
2. Choose any one of the above fragrance variations and add into the bottle.
3. Fasten the cap and shake the bottle until well combined.

Foaming Shave Soap

Ingredients and equipment:

- ½ cup liquid castile soap
- ½ cup warm distilled water
- ½ cup natural aloe Vera gel

- 2 tablespoons olive oil or almond oil
- 8 – 10 drops lavender oil or any other essential oil of your choice
- 1 teaspoon vitamin E oil
- 24 ounces pump bottle

Instructions:

1. Pour castile soap into the pump bottle. Next, add the olive oil followed by aloe Vera and distilled water.
2. Add lavender oil and vitamin E oil into the bottle.
3. Fasten the cap and shake the bottle until well combined.

Vanilla Scented Liquid Soap

Ingredients:

- 2 bars castile soap (scentless)
- 6 liters clean distilled water
- 12 drops vanilla extract
- 4 tablespoons coconut oil
- 1 large pot
- 1 cheese grater
- Dispensers

Instructions:

1. Grate the bars of soap using the cheese grater.
2. Pour water in a large pot and keep on gas for boiling.
3. When water starts boiling, add the grated soap
4. Stir well until all the soap is completely melted.
5. Remove from heat and keep aside to cool for around 8 hours.
6. It would have thickened. Now add the vanilla extract and the coconut oil and stir well.
7. For a super smooth consistency, pass through a blender.
8. Pour into dispensers.

Orange And Mint Scented Soap

Ingredients:

- ½ bar castile soap (scentless)
- 1 ½ liters clean distilled water
- 3 drops orange essential oil
- 3 drops mint essential oil
- 1 tablespoon coconut oil
- 1 large pot
- 1 cheese grater
- Dispensers

Instructions:

1. Grate the soap with the cheese grater.
2. Pour water in a large pot and place it for heating on the gas.
3. When the water starts boiling, add the soap.
4. Mix well until the soap is totally dissolved.
5. Set aside to cool and thicken for about 8 hours.
6. Now add the coconut oil, orange oil and mint oil. Stir well.
7. For a super smooth consistency pass through a blender.
8. Pour into dispensers.

Natural Homemade Baby Wash and Shampoo

Ingredients and equipment:

- 3 cups unscented liquid castile soap
- 2 – 4 teaspoons almond oil or fractionated coconut oil
- 20 drops lavender essential oil
- 8 tablespoons vegetable glycerin
- 2 teaspoons aloe Vera juice (optional)
- 2 – 4 tablespoons distilled water or filtered water
- 32 ounces pump bottle

Instructions:

1. Pour liquid soap, almond oil, aloe Vera juice and glycerin, and lavender oil into the pump bottle.
2. Pour water on top. Fasten the lid and shake the bottle for 30 – 40 seconds or until well combined.
3. Use as a wash or shampoo for babies.

Chapter 15: Hand-Milling Soap Recipes

Basic Hand-Milling Recipe, Double Boiler Method

This method is good to use until you get a slow cooker. Keep a close eye on the double boiler so it does not boil dry.

Ingredients:

- 1 pound shredded plain cold- or hot-process soap or 1-pound premade soap shreds
- 4 ounces water
- 3–6 drops food coloring
- 1 teaspoon dried herb
- 1 teaspoon fragrance oil or essential oil

Place the shreds in the top of a double boiler. Add the water and the food coloring. Cover. Place water in the bottom of the double boiler. Heat the water to boiling, then turn down to simmer. Stir gently. Avoid vigorous stirring to keep the foam level to a minimum.

Cover and cook for about 10 minutes. Don't let the boiler boil dry! Check the soap mass. It should have started to soften, and even become translucent, by now.

If it hasn't, just be patient, it will. Stir gently.

While the soap mass is heating, set out the rest of the Ingredients. Check your soap every 10 minutes or so and keep adding water to the boiler. When the soap has taken on a translucent look and you can stir the water all the way through, you are ready to make the additions. Sprinkle the herbs over the mass and stir until evenly distributed.

Remove 1/3 cup of the soap mass and place it in a warmed glass bowl. Stir the fragrance material into this and then return it to the pan and stir it in thoroughly. If you want to alter the amounts of additives, make further additions and stir well.

Scrape the soap mass into heat-resistant molds. Pack well and smooth the top. Cover with plastic wrap and let sit until soap is cooled. Turn the soap out of the mold. Cut into bars if you haven't used a bar mold. Let air-dry for a week or more, turning the bars so that they dry evenly.

Basic Hand-Milling Recipe, Slow Cooker Method

Keep checking your soap every 1/2 hour or so while the soap mass is heating.

Depending on the slow cooker and the type of soap you are using, this method can take anywhere from an hour to overnight.

You have to experiment to find out what's going to happen.
Ingredients:

- 1 pound shredded plain cold- or hot-process soap or 1-pound premade soap shreds
- 4 ounces water
- 3–6 drops food coloring
- 1 teaspoon dried herb
- 1 teaspoon fragrance oil or essential oil

Place the shreds, water, and food coloring in a slow cooker. Cover. Turn the slow cooker to its lowest setting. Let the soap mass heat in the pot for about 15 minutes, or until the pot is up to temperature. Stir gently. (Avoid vigorous stirring to keep the foam level to a minimum.) Let it cook for 30 minutes.

Check the soap mass. It may have started to soften, and even become translucent, by now. If it hasn't, just be patient; it will. Stir gently.

When the soap has taken on a translucent look and you can stir the water all the way through, you are ready to make the additions. Sprinkle the herb over the mass and stir until evenly distributed.

Remove 1/3 cup of the soap mass and place in a warmed glass bowl. Stir the fragrance material into this and then return it to the pan and stir it in thoroughly. If you want to alter the amounts of additives, make further additions and stir well.

Scrape the soap mass into heat-resistant molds.

Pack well and smooth the top. Cover with plastic wrap and let sit until soap is cooled. Turn the soap out of the mold. Cut into bars if you haven't used a bar mold. Let air-dry for a week or more, turning the bars so that they'll dry evenly.

Basic Hand-Milling Recipe, Microwave Method

Check your soap every 3 minutes while it's heating. Depending on the microwave and the type of soap you're using, this could take 15–30 minutes or more. You must experiment to know exactly what will happen.

Ingredients:

- 1 pound shredded plain cold- or hot-process soap or 1-pound premade soap shreds
- 4 ounces water
- 3-6 drops food coloring
- 1 teaspoon dried herb
- 1 teaspoon fragrance oil or essential oil

Place the shreds in a microwave-safe glass bowl. Add the water and food coloring. Stir gently. Avoid vigorous stirring to keep the foam level to a minimum. Cover with plastic wrap and place in the microwave oven. Set the microwave on medium temperature and set the cooking time to 3 minutes.

Using oven mitts, remove the bowl from the microwave. Check the soap mass. It should have started to soften, and even become translucent, by now. If it hasn't, just be patient; it will. Stir gently. Continue to heat the soap mass in intervals of 3 minutes, removing each time to check on the status. Be very careful; the soap mass will be very hot!

When the soap has taken on a translucent look and you can stir the water all the way through, you are ready to make the additions. Be very careful of escaping steam; don't stick your head over the bowl as you stir. Sprinkle the herb over the mass and stir until evenly distributed.

Remove 1/3 cup of the soap mass and place in a warmed glass bowl. Stir the fragrance material into this and then return it to the pan and stir it in thoroughly. If you want to alter the amounts of additives, make further additions and stir well.

Scrape the soap mass into heat-resistant molds. Pack well and smooth the top. Cover with plastic wrap and let sit until soap is cooled. Turn the soap out of the mold. Cut into bars if you haven't used a bar mold. Let air-dry for a week or more, turning the bars so that they'll dry evenly.

Common Mistakes

Homemade soap making lets you enjoy the exciting process of fats and lye mixed with water to create awesome bar soap. It appears almost like magic. It is a simple process to perform, but it's easy to make mistakes. Here are a few of mine.

- **Insufficient scent**

Scent oils are pricey and it's appealing to use just a little less. Recipes often don't require enough of the stinky oils, you either used oils that don't work in soap making, or you used too little fragrance if it does not smell.

- **Poor recipe**

Some recipes are just incorrect probably because the author of the recipe was ignorant about how to design soap.

- **Mistakes in measurement**

Little recipes are more challenging to solve than large ones. It is crucial to make use of the right quantities in the process of soap making. That's why recipes that use weights are better than recipes that use measuring tools like cups etc.

- **Insufficient stirring**

Different soap making recipes take different times to begin tracing or hardening as it's called.

You can design recipes that trace quickly, but in any case, you keep stirring up until the soap traces. It can take 10 minutes, or it can take hours.

- **Wrong tools**

Cutting soap is one process that can get you hurt. Attempt to get soap cutting tools, so you do not use knives to cut soap. The art part takes practice.

Conclusion

Making soap is a great pastime and can be a lucrative business. Good luck!

Made in the USA
Monee, IL
25 February 2021

61368238R00115